BEYOND PSYCHOANALYTIC LITERARY CRITICISM

Through a series of radical and innovative chapters, *Beyond Psychoanalytic Literary Criticism: Between Literature and Mind* challenges the tradition of applied psychoanalysis that has long dominated psychoanalytic literary criticism. Benjamin H. Ogden, a literary scholar, proposes that a new form of analytic literary criticism take its place, one that begins from a place of respect for the mystery of literature and the complexity of its inner workings.

In this book, through readings of authors such as J.M. Coetzee, Flannery O'Connor, and Vladimir Nabokov, the mysteries upon which literary works rely for their enduring power are enumerated and studied. Such mysteries are thereafter interwoven into a series of pioneering studies of how the conceptions of thinking, dreaming, and losing become meaningful within the unique aesthetic conditions of individual novels and poems. Each chapter is a provisional solution to the difficult "bridging problems" that arise when literary figures work in the psychoanalytic space, and when psychoanalysts attempt to make use of literature for analytic purposes.

At every turn, *Beyond Psychoanalytic Literary Criticism: Between Literature and Mind* acts as a living example of the territory it explores: the space between two disciplines, wherein the writer brings into being a form of psychoanalytic literary criticism of his own making. Forgoing traditional applied psychoanalysis and technical jargon, this highly accessible, interdisciplinary work will appeal to psychoanalysts and psychoanalytic psychotherapists, as well as literary critics and scholars.

Benjamin H. Ogden is Assistant Teaching Professor in literature and humanities at Stevens Institute of Technology. He co-authored *The Analyst's Ear and the Critic's Eye: Rethinking Psychoanalysis and Literature* with Thomas H. Ogden.

BEYOND PSYCHOANALYTIC LITERARY CRITICISM

Between Literature and Mind

Benjamin H. Ogden

Routledge
Taylor & Francis Group

LONDON AND NEW YORK

First published 2018
by Routledge
2 Park Square, Milton Park, Abingdon, Oxon OX14 4RN

and by Routledge
711 Third Avenue, New York, NY 10017

Routledge is an imprint of the Taylor & Francis Group, an informa business

© 2018 Benjamin H. Ogden

Library of Congress Cataloging in Publication Data
Names: Ogden, Benjamin H.
Title: Beyond psychoanalytic literary criticism : between literature and mind / Benjamin H. Ogden.
Description: London ; New York, NY : Routledge, 2018. | Includes bibliographical references and index.
Identifiers: LCCN 2017054387 (print) | LCCN 2017059048 (ebook) | ISBN 9781351234382 (Master) | ISBN 9781351234375 (Web PDF) | ISBN 9781351234368 (ePub) | ISBN 9781351234351 (Mobipocket/Kindle) | ISBN 9780815377276 (hardback : alk. paper) | ISBN 9780815377283 (pbk. : alk. paper)
Subjects: LCSH: Psychoanalysis and literature. | Literature--History and criticism.
Classification: LCC PN56.P92 (ebook) | LCC PN56.P92 O57 2018 (print) | DDC 801/.92–dc23
LC record available at https://lccn.loc.gov/2017054387

ISBN: 978-0-8153-7727-6 (hbk)
ISBN: 978-0-8153-7728-3 (pbk)
ISBN: 978-1-3512-3438-2 (ebk)

Typeset in Bembo
by Taylor & Francis Books

For Leah

CONTENTS

PART IV
Brief interlude 99

PART V
Neither out far nor in deep 105

PERMISSIONS/ACKNOWLEDGMENTS

Every effort has been made to contact the copyright holders for their permission to reprint selections of this book for which it was deemed necessary. Routledge would be grateful to hear from any copyright holder who is not here acknowledged and we will undertake to rectify any errors or omissions in future editions of this book. The author would like to thank the following copyright holders for permission to reuse the previously published essays and quotations listed below:

Introduction

Excerpts are taken from "The Lost Son," copyright © 1947 by Theodore Roethke. Copyright © 1966 and renewed 1994 by Beatrice Lushington; from *Collected Poems* by Theodore Roethke. Used by permission of Doubleday, an imprint of the Knopf Doubleday Publishing Group, a division of Penguin Random House LLC. All rights reserved.

Chapter 1

Chapter one first published as "The risk of true confession: On literature and mystery," *Fort da* 23.1: 40–61, May 2017. Copyright *fort da*. Reprinted by kind permission of the journal.

Excerpts from "Parker's Back" from *The Complete Stories* by Flannery O'Connor, copyright © 1971 by the Estate of Mary Flannery O'Connor. Also reprinted by permission of Farrar, Straus & Giroux.

Excerpts from *Life and Times of Michael K* by J.M. Coetzee, copyright © 1983 by J.M. Coetzee. Used by permission of Viking Books, an imprint of Penguin Publishing Group, a division of Penguin Random House LLC. All rights reserved.

Chapter 2

Chapter 3

Chapter 4

by the President and Fellows of Harvard College. Copyright © renewed 1979, 1983 by the President and Fellows of Harvard College. Copyright © 1914, 1918, 1919, 1924, 1929, 1930, 1932, 1935, 1937, 1942 by Martha Dickinson Bianchi. Copyright © 1952, 1957, 1958, 1963, 1965 by Mary L. Hampson.

Excerpts from *Never Let Me Go* by Kazuo Ishiguro, copyright © 2005 by Kazuo Ishiguro. Used by permission of Alfred A. Knopf, an imprint of the Knopf Doubleday Publishing Group, a division of Penguin Random House LLC. All rights reserved.

Chapter 5

Excerpt from *The Birds* by Tarjei Vesaas, republished by kind permission of Archipelago Books. All rights reserved.

Chapter 7

Excerpts from "On Exactitude in Science," copyright © 1998 by Maria Kodama; translation copyright © 1998 by Penguin Random House LLC; from *Collected Fictions: Volume 3* by Jorge Luis Borges, translated by Andrew Hurley. Used by permission of Viking Books, an imprint of Penguin Publishing Group, a division of Penguin Random House LLC. All rights reserved.

Excerpts from "The Poem That Can't Be Written" from *The History of Forgetting* by Lawrence Raab, copyright © 2009 by Lawrence Raab. Used by permission of Penguin Books, an imprint of Penguin Publishing Group, a division of Penguin Random House LLC. All rights reserved.

Excerpts from *The Eternal Husband and Other Stories* by Fyodor Dostoevsky.

Translated by Richard Pevear and Larissa Volokhonsky, translation copyright © 1997 by Richard Pevear and Larissa Volokhonsky. Used by permission of Bantam Books, an imprint of Random House, a division of Penguin Random House LLC. All rights reserved.

Chapter 8

Chapter 8 first published as "Inside the magic circle: On Homero Aridjis' *The Child Poet*" in the newsletter of the Psychoanalytic Institute of Northern California, May 2017. Excerpts from *The Child Poet* by Homero Aridjis republished by permission of Archipelago Books. All rights reserved.

Acknowledgements

The author would like to thank Giuseppe Civitarese, Alberto Rocha Barros, Elias Rocha Barros, and Elizabeth Rocha Barros for their kindness, support, and friendship, without which this book would not have been written.

PREFACE

The essays in this book constitute my effort over the past four years to explore new ways in which literature and psychoanalysis can be brought into conversation with one another, and to address, more broadly, the challenges and rewards of inter-disciplinary writing and thinking (Ogden 2013, 2014, 2016, 2017a, 2017b). I have not gone about exploring these issues by presenting a single, sustained argument in support of any particular vision of how two fields must come together. I could not supply any such vision even if I had a desire to, for the act of writing itself is a kind of truth-seeking, and each time I write, the truth I am after is formed by the unique conditions and goals of that period of writing, and of that particular project. What is true in one chapter of this book is untrue in another, because the respec-tive chapters are trying to achieve different ends, or meant to test the value of different lines of thinking. In that respect, this book is an experiment, as all life is an experiment. The poet WB Yeats spoke of the feeling of completing a poem as the feeling of a jewel box snapping shut. These essays are nine different boxes that I hope have snapped shut.

In this book, I am not writing about the topic of psychoanalysis and literature from the outside, but from within, reimagining *as a writer* the nature of each field in a different way in each chapter. As such, each chapter is a coming into being of the very conversation I wish to explore. Sometimes, as in the Introduction, the approach takes an unorthodox form, as I there bring together an idea drawn from the psychoanalyst Wilfred Bion with the narrative structure of experimental fiction. Although this introduction serves as a commentary on the state one finds oneself in when trying to work in an interdisciplinary way, it is intended as a living example of the struggle to do justice to whichever fields one draws upon for one's work, not as a reflection on the theoretical origins of the struggle.

To address the challenges of interdisciplinary work, the book examines the "bridging problems" that arise when a specific novelist or psychoanalyst tries to extend the reach of their writing and thinking into the other discipline. To explore this phenomenon, which of course has a very long history, I first consider the path from literature to psychoanalysis. Chapter 2 reviews *The Good Story: Exchanges on Truth, Fiction, and Psychoanalytic Psychotherapy* (Coetzee and Kurtz 2015), an extensive email correspondence between the novelist J.M. Coetzee and the psychoanalyst Arabella Kurtz. Much like many of the essays in this book, *The Good Story* lives out an ongoing struggle to see more clearly the inner-workings of interdisplinary thinking and writing, and finds in the redemptive and therapeutic potential of narrative a beginning point for redrawing the boundary between literature and psychoanalysis. Still, even in Coetzee and Kurtz's attempt to create a dialogue that is alive to what is most important to both fields, their correspondence also brings into focus the pitfalls of interdisciplinary work, which I draw out at some length. I am particularly fond of the chapter on *The Good Story*, which constitutes a discussion between a literary scholar and a practicing analyst, much as my previous book, *The Analyst's Ear and the Critic's Eye: Rethinking Psychoanalysis and Literature* (Ogden and Ogden 2013), was a conversation (held through the *we* pronoun we used to present our ideas, both when they differed and when they overlapped) between myself, a widely published literary scholar (Ogden 2009, 2010, 2012a, 2012b, 2013, 2014), and my father, Thomas H. Ogden, who has practiced and written about psychoanalysis for the last forty years.

As a companion piece, the subsequent chapter reverses course: instead of a novelist like Coetzee heading out into psychoanalytic waters, I look at an analyst testing his hand at couching psychoanalytic theory in fictional terms. I am speaking of Wilfred Bion's *A Memoir of the Future*, which is a fascinating nightmare of a book, one that highlights both the brilliance of Bion's theory of thinking and the challenges of finding it a natural home in fiction. To illustrate this challenge, I bring Coetzee back into the mix by looking at how he envisions thinking, and the coming into being of literary truth, in the opening of his novel *Elizabeth Costello*. In so doing, I wonder at what Coetzee could teach Bion about the business of producing fiction.

In chapters 4, 5, 6, and 7, I deal expressly with how concerns that have always been central to psychoanalysis (specifically, thinking, losing, and dreaming) are explored in a range of literary works. But "explored" here does not quite say what I am trying to do in these essays. In actual fact, underlying nearly everything in this book is a feeling that, in works of psychoanalytic literary criticism, works of literature are often reduced to psychoanalysis. What I mean by this is that literature is used as a tool for illustrating psychoanalytic concepts and ideas, which has the effect of stealing from literature the mystery upon which it relies to be meaningful as literature. In chapter 9 I address, in detail, why I find the use of literature for psychoanalytic discussion problematic, and, in chapter 1, why literature cannot be treated in this way without damaging a mystery that is indispensable to it. Suffice it to say here that my readings of literature try to speak to psychoanalytic issues from a psychoanalytic sensibility informed by psychoanalytic readings but without using psychoanalytic terminology to excess. For that reason, essays in this book will contain relatively little psychoanalytic terminology; rather, they aspire to engage with psychoanalysis in any way other than theoretical formulations. This may strike the reader as unusual, or even dismissive of psychoanalysis, but as I said I am interested in inventing a form of engagement between the aliveness of literature and the aliveness of analysis that does not require specialized theory. This would be a form of writing between disciplines, not forcing an intersection of disciplines.

I say "between disciplines" as if it were a secondary space, a subset of the proper disciplines. Winnicott has a wonderful phrase in "The Place Where We Live": "I wish to examine the place, using the word in an abstract sense, where we most of the time are when we are experiencing life" (1971, p. 104). This place "where we most of the time are" is where I am trying to work in this book. Where is this? Between disciplines, I would say. I could also express this as: outside of any given discipline. Most of the time we are not practicing a certain branch of knowledge. Rather, we are calling upon all we know and feel to do the job at hand. We are working in a place where no one kind of knowledge will do. How is this? If I am running, I am not doing physics, or biology, or aesthetics. I am running. In order to run, physics is not enough; nor is biology; nor is aesthetics, nor is psychology or anthropology. Nor is even the combination of them all. Though a clearer picture of running will emerge if we use many branches of knowledge, we still in that case will only be replacing running with the intersection of many different forms of description and explanation. But if I wish to understand running—to think about it in the moment—I must work in the space between these many disciplines where running is happening. This space belongs to no single discipline, nor even an amalgamation of several disciplines. This is the place where we most of the time are: trying to understand the runner as he runs. Where we most of the time are is where our understanding of who we are as literary scholars or psychoanalysts should begin, for it is really a shared point of origin. This undifferentiated matrix is common to us, and only afterwards do we break out into camps.

At bottom, this book is an attempt to reflect on this space as I work within it, and to do so in a way that is nearly free of specialized terminology that would push the thinking back into one intellectual tradition or another. This is my way of speaking in a voice that has within it the "oversound" (Frost, 1942, p. 308) of orthodox disciplines but a timbre that I hope is that of an independent thinker.

INTRODUCTION

Between the rails: An allegory of art, science and many other things

Suppose, as Bion does on the first page of *Transformations* (1965), that we stand between two railroad lines that extend into the distance as far as the eye can see. The lines will be seen to converge at the horizon. Where we stand, the lines cannot converge, for we separate them by standing between them. Put as a rule, so long as we are between the lines, the lines will not converge where we are.

If we set out to find the point at which the railroad lines cross by walking up the lines, we will be disappointed. The lines do not converge; or, we are never *not* between the lines. Not only do we, even after the longest periods of trekking, not find the hoped-for point of intersection, but the lines themselves never even encourage us one bit by drawing closer together. It is as if the lines wanted to keep us marching on, but never to make us any promises. What's more, it is as if the lines had contrary purposes in this world: to beguile us and to mock us; to make us observe a bond at which we could plausibly arrive and to keep us from confirming a bond.

Who are we but Sisyphus? each of us begins to think privately.

At some point in time, we lose hope. Defeated, we decide to reclaim our lives. We choose to turn back, plugging our ears to the siren song of the railroad lines.

And upon turning around, what do we see? A point of convergence in the distance, of course. Back there, behind us, in the past: however you want to put it, the lines now appear to converge there, and not only do they converge, but I am convinced—and I believe you are as well—that the lines appear to cross at the very point from which we had initially set out on our journey between the tracks.

Hopeful, we hurry back (which is now forward) toward the point of intersection, doubly happy that we will not only have found the meeting point but be home as well. The intersection will mark a homecoming.

And upon returning home, what do we, who walk between Art and Science, find?

So long as we are between the lines, the lines will not converge. Space will separate Field of Study One from Field of Study Two.

A strange change takes place following our journey out and back. Before leaving on our excursion, had you asked us if the railroad tracks were close to one another, we would have said, "Yes, indeed, just a few feet separate the lines." One of us may even have demonstrated that if one stretches one's legs out far enough to either side one person can almost, quite nearly, touch a foot to each rail. A very tall or flexible person could likely do it. The point being: closing the gap had once felt to us like a small matter, the simplest of bridging problems.

But upon returning, we are both overcome by the same feeling of despair: the rails are so very far apart now. They may as well be an eternity apart or a million light years. Our curiosity transforms into a nameless dread. No longer do we dream of intersection. Our only thought is of the chasm in which we now stand. We think of nothing else.

To occupy ourselves, to keep from going mad, we take walks, lasting months or even years, in the direction of the point in the distance where, our eyes tell us, Psychoanalysis and Literature touch, where there is no longer a discernible distance between one and the other.

We never get there. Our expeditions become an affront to us. Better than doing nothing, we say to ourselves.

But is it really? There must be better ways of wasting time. We are getting older out here.

One night, I awake to find you on top of me, straddling me, your hands on my neck. I am being choked. You want me dead.

In defense, to preserve myself, I roll on top of you. The reversal is an excitement for both of us. We make love.

Why? we both wonder afterward, heaving between the railroad tracks. What have we, our pleasure or our annihilation, to do with these rails? They were there when we got here. Won't they be here when we are gone, whatever we think of them?

For months, nightly, this ritual repeats itself. Despite the intensity of it, it appears to change nothing.

In due course, our belief in a place where the lines converge where we are all but vanishes. If the lines do indeed converge somewhere, somewhere will always be a long way to go.

The effects of loss of faith are terrible and grow worse each day. We become despondent in the most dramatic style: all life is a curse. The stars are bizarre objects. God forgets us. The horizon is pure mockery. Poets are quoted loudly and in earnest.

We chant: Snail, snail, glister me forward, Bird, soft-sigh me home, Worm be with me. This is our hard time.[1]

Imagine now that, in these circumstances, to one of us an idea presents itself. It is a simple idea, but appears a good one. (Whether the idea comes to you or me is of no consequence ultimately, though the debates between us proceed interminably.) The idea is this: build something. Specifically, build a wall.

If we cannot find where the lines meet, so the idea goes, it is best to fill up the intervening space between the lines ourselves.

What sense is there in doing such a thing? What ails us, we have learned from our years between the tracks, is the point of intersection that we can see at the horizon, our knowledge that, whenever we go out in search of this convergence, we cannot find it, and worse still, upon turning around, we find the convergence at a place where our experience tells us it cannot be (our homeland, our place of birth).

So, let us block out the horizon that so torments us.

If what we build is wide enough (it stretches from rail to rail) and high enough (we cannot see over it or climb up it), and if we construct it so that no light can pass through it, then our problem—that convergence we always perceive way out there—will no longer be visible to us. The result? The lines will seem *to us* to converge at the wall itself. If nothing beyond the wall is visible, there will be no suggestion of any distant point at which the lines touch. The wall will make the lines seem to converge by eliminating the perspective from which they appear to converge but never do. We build a wall, in other words, not so that the lines will in fact converge, but so that the perspective from which they never converge (but seem to) will be concealed by our creation.

There is only one catch, easily managed: for the wall to serve its intended purpose, the observer must forget that the lines continue beyond the wall, but *remember his desire for an intersection* (remember always that behind him are lines in search of a convergence). If he cannot forget that behind the wall parallel lines converge in the distance, he will know that the wall is merely a screen hiding behind it the promise of true intersection; if he cannot desire the meeting of the lines, the wall will seem only like a dead-end for parallel lines, and will have no significance. He must retain desire, but lose memory.

If the observer (in this case, you and I) can forget and remember in this way, the observer will be satisfied, even thrilled, with what we have built. He will have, at long last, his convergence.

We ourselves would have been quite satisfied to find such an ending on any one of our former journeys.

Dirt is plentiful between the railroad tracks, so it is with dirt that we begin to build. In no time, using just our hands, we have a pile. The pile quickly becomes a mound, and shortly thereafter, the mound a larger mound. It looks as if dirt will serve our every purpose. The sky is quite literally the limit.

Before long, the mound is so large it really does block out the horizon. What we have made is not quite a mountain, could not even be called a hill, but it is unquestionably an ample Tower.

Humble though it may be, to we who built it, the Tower is celestial; it is as if the moon had moved in front of the sun. Enthralled, practically cooing, we lie in our moon's shade. We give it all our attention, relieved to be able to look in a direction that once only hung frustration before our eyes. We pat at the slope of it tenderly where it erodes, knowing that maintenance is as necessary as innovation.

But dirt is easily blown about. In the morning, you wake me and point: half of the heap is scattered. We can rebuild it, surely, but there is nothing to keep the winds—which are controlled by the gods—from chopping the head off of our dirt Tower every night. We are no Scheherazade.

We have no choice but to count the Tower a failure.

Though outwardly we blame the wind for our ruin, the truth is that our Tower was a gaffe, wind or no wind. For the Tower reminded us of the point of intersection behind it. Try as we did to forget that fact, that dirt heap was not a wall, but a window through which our mind's eye could see the horizon, and at it the point at which we could see our lines touch.

You asked me one day, as we were pushing the last of the Tower down: what was it about the Tower that reminded us of what lay behind it?

It looks like a lie, I told you. It serves no purpose. It is ugly, with all the charm of a prostitute. Why else would it be here, of all places, if it were not a pale, provisional alternative to true connection?

The dirt is cleared away. Time passes. As is usually the case, substantive change comes during the night, while I am asleep, swelling with dream.

One morning I awake to find you coming toward me down the tracks, a box of tools in one hand, a bundle of materials under an armpit. You drop all of it in front of me, triumphant.

Work begins immediately and continues through the day, until with no light at all work is pointless. Despite the wind we enjoy ourselves—we have more fun with the lumber, the joists and nails, and the different liquid adhesives than we ever had with dirt.

Once finished, we see the problem immediately. Perceived at a distance, the horizon is eclipsed, boarded up perfectly. But, upon approach and looking closely, holes and cracks begin to show. Light streams through a seam, or pours through a nearly imperceptible flaw like a yellow shoelace being fed through a keyhole. Peeking through these breaks, we catch glimpses of one or the other rail. Both rails are seldom visible simultaneously, and the point where they meet is mostly hidden from view. But glimpses of each are enough to ruin all. Even one crack is a failure, which makes our second creation as ineffectual as our first.

Suppose, during dead of night, while still asleep, I venture out. Some hours later, by morning time, I return with a blank canvas, one as wide as the railroad lines and as tall as the dirt Tower had ever been. It is opaque, as we had wished. Where exactly I had found such a canvas neither of us can say.

There would be, of course, the problem of hanging the canvas. But let us suppose that we solve this problem, and having solved this problem push forward. The canvas is hung, we can no longer see the horizon, there isn't a single hole or crack in the canvas, and we learn to forget what is beyond the canvas.

And indeed, we are for some time thrilled by this solution. For that is exactly what it appears to be: an end to our problems and therefore the resumption of a proper life. Our depression soon subsides. A whole part of my inner world returns to me. I recall, with a kind of tender ferocity, what I had always wanted to be when I grew up: a general repairman, so that I could work on anything that could possibly break, which would make me a useful worker always in demand. Furthermore, while the smallest individual unit had always been one person, now it is two people, you and me, between whom there grows fellow feeling.

If I could have kept it that way forever, even at a great cost to the rest of humanity, I would have certainly done so. I was becoming the kind of person who does not mind being selfish.

But it did not last, this hunger for life. For one morning (always the morning, I do not believe any longer that we had middays) I come out of dream to discover that you have made a mark upon the canvas. You have mixed dirt with a little spittle, pushed the tip of a small stick into the mixture, and with this mud drawn a single line in the lower-left quadrant of the canvas.

I have no grounds for objection to what you have done, but we both know at once that all is lost. With a heave, you throw the stick over the canvas and kick dirt atop the ink you had made. You give me your back, though it is with yourself that you are furious. Embarrassed, you do not speak to me for a long time.

I am not angry with you, though. This was going to happen; I had had the same instinct myself, though had beaten it back more successfully than you. To make you feel better, I add my own disordered markings on the canvas. We even find some pleasure, though not much, in our pointless decorations. In this way we resume the life we had briefly abandoned.

Years pass, a time during which I forget and remember the horizon in alternation. My dreams are awash in intersections, as are yours, you confide. We consider tearing the canvas down, and heading again to the horizon, to the meeting of the lines. Even if it takes us the rest of our lives, it is better to arrive with no time left than live long days burdened by unmet dreams. Perhaps this was only a part of the madness that gripped us.

There can be no doubt that we would have died this way had we not discovered that we had an eraser with us. As it is, the dust with which we had built the Tower those many years ago was so finely ground and soft to touch that when rubbed upon the canvas the mud would fall away, leaving the canvas as white as new. The eraser, we learned, is a much greater invention than the pen. The blank canvas appeased us for a long time afterward.

Sooner or later, however, the empty canvas becomes an object of persecution. Its blankness reminds us of what goes on behind it, which could be anything at all, even something inscrutable or unexpected, but which most likely was that very distant point of intersection that no surveyor (not even one of mind, body, and heart) would find, but that was, finally, in its own way, there.

So early one day, in a fit of something (love? mystery? courage?), we mix our spit in with the dirt, take up sticks and dip them into the mixture, and upon the blank canvas we draw the intersection we had been in search of all those years. I draw a line, and you draw a line. We work like bandits on these simple lines. Once drawn, the lines intersect right where we are, and it is as if an infinite gap had shrunk to nothing. And very easily, now, we remember that the lines wanted to converge and that beyond this canvas nothing else existed, and here is the real convergence that the world had kept from us. We had our solution.

The following morning, we are awoken by voices. Still half-asleep, we scrabble to our feet, throwing off the heavy blanket we share on lonely nights. We dare not speak. We had thought it was only the two of us between the lines.

Once the rubble of sleep is cleared from our eyes, we see them: a man and a woman (or what looked to me like a woman, though her head was bandaged with gauze, and her shirt so billowy that I could not tell if it hid breasts or the slack belly of a man). They ignore us. The woman, taking the lead while the man watches, runs a gloved hand over the converging lines drawn on the canvas. She makes sounds not words. The sounds are at first quizzical. Shortly, they acquire over-sounds of frustration (huffing, grunting, wheezing, and so on and so forth). The man, now contributing, hurls a handful of dirt against the canvas. Nothing. He takes a stick (concealed within the long jacket he wears) and beats the canvas mightily. The canvas billows but does not tear.

The man and woman do not stop their attempt to destroy the canvas. Under a barrage, the canvas shakes like madness; then, a cry to the heavens, and the man's arm plunges through the skin of the canvas with a punch. The small, fist-sized hole is quickly enlarged by both man and woman; in a matter of seconds, long strips have been removed from the canvas in every direction from the original hole. This must have weakened the entire structure, for with a single tug, the entire canvas falls from its moorings. Not satisfied, the man takes up the canvas in his arms and tosses it beyond the lines.

I look at the man, and he sees the question in my eyes.

—We are here to find the link, nothing else.

—The link?

—The point where there is no longer space between the lines. We see it always in the distance, but have yet to come upon it.

They are us, we think. Half our age, but us all the same. We try to explain to them what we have learned, that the intersection never comes so long as you are between the lines. The only hope, we tell them, is to block out the horizon and draw in the convergence for yourself, as we had done. The intersection (the link, as they call it) that you had thought you were approaching was in fact only our rendering of intersection. We point to the horizon, where, with the canvas gone, we can see the convergence: where you want to be is as far away as ever.

To befriend them, perhaps even to preserve ourselves, we offer them refuge where we are. It will be nice to be four, not two, we propose. Less lonely. You can help us construct a better canvas, one that cannot be torn down.

They have no interest in companionship or canvases. Without another word, they push past us, heading toward the link they see, and with which they are wholeheartedly in love.

The last word the man speaks to us is *liars*.

A long night's sleep and I awake to find you clutching another canvas, along with all the tools one needs to hang it. Rebuilding is a breeze. We repeat the process, but at each step we are more careful. Our concern now is with building a canvas that will withstand an attack. The nails are driven deeper and straighter; the bolts given an additional quarter turn; the convergence drawn with a ruler instead of freehand. We hope not to have another Tower on our hands.

The next morning, we awake to find the canvas is already destroyed. A group of women with scissors and knives have cut it out of its moorings. They laugh at us; one spits upon me. We call after them, trying to explain their error, but they push on.

This ritual repeats itself. First the building, then the tearing down by others, then the mockery and anger and bemusement at our rendering. We continue living like this, we both know, only because we are out of ideas.

Perhaps, we begin to think, our problem is that we had not gone far enough, had not searched for long enough, had not sacrificed everything that we could have (you kept a handful of beetroot seeds, I a pouch of tomato seeds). Yes, that has to be it. So we pack the little we have into our pockets and go once again in the direction of intersection. Once again, we make love in the night. Months pass.

Until, one day, we see ahead of us what appears to be the intersection. Still a bit of a distance off, but unmistakably nearer to us. Never had it appeared so close, so attainable. We hurry ahead, eyes filled with tears of joy, never closer the whole rest of our lives.

But when we arrive, we arrive at a canvas, one much like ours, with an intersection drawn (rather crudely, I thought) on the surface. At our feet, two men and two women sleep. One of the women is clearly pregnant. Their skin is darker than ours, and not only because of the hot sun under which they have lived their lives.

When they awake, they begin to speak to us in a language we cannot understand. Despite the barrier between our languages, it is obvious we are unwanted. I make a motion—the way mimes do—to join their group, to become a larger force. The man—the one with the child on the way, I gather—holds a knife up at me. So, having no choice, we tear down their canvas and push on.

At certain points in the future, exhausted from destroying canvases, we would resort to building our own again: getting the materials, hanging the canvas, drawing the convergence of the railroad lines so that they intersected where we stood. In this way, for stretches of time, we could imagine we were alone, that our intersection was there next to us, that it would last forever, or at least beyond our lifetimes. In no time, naturally, it was gone. Then, on our feet again, it was off into the horizon.

And things just sort of went on like this.

Note

1 This chant is from Theodore Roethke's poem "The Lost Son" (1948/1975).

PART I

Mysteries exchanged for words

1

THE RISK OF TRUE CONFESSION

On literature and mystery[1]

Confessional literature is a kind of autobiographical writing in which one tries to tell the truth of oneself, about oneself, as honestly and completely as one can. We should think that confession, above all other modes of literary representation, would come closest to reporting the truth, for it is based on several things that tend to guarantee the truth from human beings: a desire to unburden oneself of pain and shame; the confessor's fear of the consequences of mendacity; and it is spoken to a God whom the confessor desires to know and serve and elicit the forgiveness of—in other words, the confessor has the listener he wants, a listener who is both all-powerful and prepared to forgive.

Confession, we might say, meets the conditions for truth. It posits individual man as the hero of his own life, able to know the contents of his own heart and the nature of his own desires, but it does so within the context of an inviolable religious principle, which is that the smallest individual unit is not one person, but two people—God and yourself, or if you don't believe in God, whichever Sovereign Judge your confession is addressed to. For this reason, the confession has produced some of the most important works of Western literature: St. Augustine's *Confessions*, of course, but also the modern confessions of Wordsworth's *The Prelude* and Rousseau's *The Confessions*, which are notable for having been among the first works of literature to "lay stress on the significance of childhood experience" (Rousseau, 1996, "Intro," p. ix) in forming the adult personality.

So, from the outside looking in, confession—which might also go under the name of autobiography—appears to be as devoted to the truth as writing can be. In fact, "Autobiography is usually thought of not as a kind of fiction-writing but as a kind of history-writing, with the same allegiance to the truth as history has" (Coetzee, 1984). The reader is, of course, familiar with the limitations of self-knowledge and self-expression; try as hard as one can, one may still not tell the truth about oneself. But this does not detract from the essential nature of the confessional genre—yes, it can be misused, but it is nonetheless essentially *truth-directed* (Coetzee, 1992, p. 261).

But, we might ask, does this hold true if we look at confession *from the inside*, that is, if we look at it from the perspective of the writer of confession, of one like Rousseau? J.M. Coetzee has written on this subject—the subject of the relationship between confessional writing and the truth—on a number of occasions. For the moment, my focus will be on his essay "Truth in Autobiography," which is little known and difficult to find outside South Africa, having been delivered as a short commencement address at the University of Cape Town in 1984. In it, Coetzee examines the confession from the perspective of the writer, and in the process gestures toward a central fact about how literature works, the obscure source of its power.

In "Truth in Autobiography," Coetzee argues that confessional literature is predicated on a particular kind of economy, a system of exchange in which concealed truths are of the greatest value, and in which an author cannot afford to reveal all his truth because, if he does, the mode of confession must come to an end. To make this point, Coetzee dissects a story Rousseau tells about himself in *The Confessions*. A young Rousseau, with enough money to do so, wishes to buy a cake, yet, Rousseau writes, "Everywhere I am intimidated, restrained by some obstacle or other. I return home consumed with longing yet not having the courage to buy anything" (p. 35). Rousseau resorts to stealing the cake, and then claims that the shameful truth underlying the theft is that, by a peculiarity of nature, he is possessed by both the greatest avarice and an overwhelming "contempt for money."

But, as Coetzee points out, that explanation may not satisfy us, and as readers we are free to look for further explanations. For instance, as readers we are led to believe that procuring the cake does not in the end satisfy Rousseau's desire for cake—it curbs his appetite but is only a provisional solution to a far more elemental struggle against desire.

What has happened is that Rousseau has revealed a truth, but not necessarily *the* truth; he has kept a certain truth in reserve. Even though Rousseau claims he has confessed the truth of the incident, we still do not know the truth of what the cake stands for, what it symbolizes within Rousseau's psychology. About this, Coetzee writes:

> We begin to see now why Rousseau cannot *afford* to carry his investigations further than he does; why, having offered us a glimpse of his peculiarity, he must retract it, wrap it up again. Time after time … Rousseau performs the double movement of offering to spend one of his mysterious contradictions, then withdrawing it, in order to maintain the freedom which, in his system, belong to those who hold their assets in reserve. If you take away the last veil and are left with no mystery, no further confession is necessary. The risk of true confession is therefore not to the self but to the life of the medium. If you

reveal the inner operations of the economy of confession, you kill the goose that lays the golden eggs.

p.3

With this, we see Coetzee's essential insight about the nature of autobiography. Autobiography is a genre in which the author must be in search of an essential truth about the self; discovering truths about the self requires self-doubt, self-doubt being the means by which we distinguish between superficial and essential truths. However, autobiography as a medium, as an economy, works by *concealing* truths. Autobiography must keep in reserve certain truths, must not unearth every truth, for if it does then the medium itself will come to an end. Outwardly, auto-biography is a noble pursuit of the truth; inwardly, it refrains from discovering, or articulating, certain truths as a way of remaining operative. The dirty secret of autobiography is that, while it claims to pursue an essential truth about the self, it is, in fact, at every moment concerned with not discovering too much truth, *not* delivering on the very thing it promises. As Coetzee remarks of Rousseau's vexation with the cake:

> So the cake is stolen and eaten *and* the value of the desire for it (if not the desire itself) is retained. It is retained as a resource which, to the degree that it is mysterious, fascinating, illicit, shameful, can be exchanged for words in the economy of confession.
>
> *p. 3*

Coetzee has said that "all autobiography is storytelling, all writing is auto-biography" (1992, p. 391); by this logic, whatever he has said about confession is also true of all forms of literary writing. The question is: what has Coetzee revealed about the nature of fiction writing? I believe it is this: literature is founded not on truth, but on mystery. What is of value to the writer is not the truths he arrives at or reveals, but the secrets and mysteries he retains within the economy of confes-sion. Literature does not end with the truth; it ends where mystery runs out. Therefore, the writer's concern as he writes—Rousseau's concern as he confesses—is with the creation of mystery, with the generation of unknowns that can be, as Coetzee puts it, "exchanged for words." In this sense, the author writes—and perhaps the reader reads—not to know more, but to know less, for literature sur-vives only so long as it contains mystery, and it seems that the mysteries of great literature are limitless, inexhaustible, not by genius but by design.

This raises the important matter of how writers create the mystery upon which the value and interest of their writing rests. While every writer creates mystery in one way or another, I think we can see that different authors write mystery in different ways. This is the subject of the remainder of this paper: the ways in which writers create the mystery on which the life of their work is staked. The three forms of mystery that I have identified as central to writers are the *mystery of looking, the mystery of thinking*, and the *mystery of language*. I will take them in that order, using a single author in each case to exemplify what I mean by that particular kind of mystery.

The mystery of looking

"For the writer of fiction everything has its testing point in the eye, and the eye is an organ that eventually involves the whole of the personality, and as much of the world as can be got into it" (1969, p. 144). This is Flannery O'Connor, speaking about the role of vision in her art. O'Connor is one of 20th-century America's three greatest short story writers, the other two being (in my estimation) John Cheever and Ernest Hemingway. She was born in 1925 and raised in Savannah, Georgia, in the center of the Bible Belt, a vast swathe of the American South that is deeply, proudly Protestant. O'Connor was raised as, and would remain all her life, deeply, unabashedly Catholic. Her Catholicism is at the center of the moral vision of her writing. Central to her works is her relationship to the oftentimes grotesque and devilish American South, how her Catholic notions of grace penetrate into deeply sordid lives that are otherwise divorced from Catholic spirituality. Many of her stories involve humorous, desperate, and ludicrous pursuits of salvation, oftentimes culminating in moments of unexpected, even unwarranted, grace. Her subject was, as she put it, "the action of grace in territory held largely by the devil" (p. 118).

In 1937, O'Connor's father was diagnosed with lupus, a disease that ultimately killed him when O'Connor was 15 years old, leaving her inconsolable. At 21 years old she left Georgia for Iowa, where should would attend the prestigious Iowa Writers Workshop, and where she would begin to write several of the stories that form her first novel, *Wise Blood* (1952). Then in 1951, not long after her schooling in Iowa was complete, O'Connor was diagnosed with lupus, the same condition that had killed her father. Due to illness, she returned to Georgia, and spent the rest of her life living with her mother in the small town of Midgeville, never marrying or having children, a virgin, and writing consistently. Lupus left her with enough energy to write for two hours each day; with her remaining strength she raised a prolific number of birds, including several dozen peafowl. O'Connor managed to last 14 years with lupus, nine more than the doctors gave her. But it killed her at the age of 39. She was a hard worker, writing up to the very end of her life, hiding stories under her pillow so the doctors wouldn't take them away from her, and editing her final stories after taking last rites.

The world was fundamentally mysterious to Flannery O'Connor because she was a Catholic; because she not only believed in God but saw him everywhere. Her stories were not Catholic because she saw with the eyes of the Church, or because her stories put forward good Christian morals—that sort of Christian writing she detested. Rather, O'Connor's stories were Catholic because she reported what she saw, and what she saw was a world replete with the Christian mysteries. This made her job easier, for, being a devout Catholic, mystery was built into her life, into her way of seeing. She didn't have to invent mystery, or find it; all she had to do was record it. O'Connor (1969, p. 31) writes:

In the greatest fiction, the writer's moral sense coincides with his dramatic sense, and I see no way for it to do this unless his moral judgment is part of the very act of seeing, and he is free to use it. I have heard it said that Christian dogma is a hindrance to the writer, but I myself have found nothing further from the truth. Actually, it frees the storyteller to observe. It is not a set of rules which fixes what he sees in the world. It affects his writing primarily by guaranteeing his respect for mystery.

Writing demands mystery, and O'Connor counts herself fortunate not to have to worry about creating any from scratch, for her Catholicism guarantees all the mystery she needs; all she must do is observe it.

Elsewhere, O'Connor says:

The beginning of human knowledge is through the senses, and the fiction writer begins where human perception begins. He appeals through the senses, and you cannot appeal to the sense with abstractions. It is a good deal easier for most people to state an abstract idea than to describe and thus re-create some object that they actually see. But the world of the fiction writer is full of matter, and this is what the beginning fiction writers are very loath to create. They are concerned primarily with unfleshed ideas and emotions. They are apt to be reformers and to want to write because they are possessed not by a story but by the bare bones of some abstract notion. They are conscious of problems, not of people, of questions and issues, not of the texture of existence, of case histories and of everything that has a sociological smack, instead of with all those concrete details of life that make actual the mystery of our position on earth.

p. 68

Of course, in recording what she sees near to her, O'Connor also records what is very far away, and also very deep inside. She records the relationship between the physical world we live in—a world that on the surface can seem profoundly incompatible with the Christian God—and those immutable, "ultimate concerns" that make up life—matters of the spirit and of eternity. She documents the relationship between the physical world (what is explainable) and those mysterious moments when her characters are "forced out to meet evil and grace and … act on a trust beyond themselves—whether they know very clearly what it is they act upon or not" (p. 42).

For O'Connor it was not enough simply to record the world as she experienced it, for as she realized, the audience that read her fiction could not see as she did. She had to *distort* the world so that her reader (a Northern reader generally) could see too. The most extreme of these distortions results in characters that are generally referred to as grotesque. The grotesque is a hallmark of the literature of the American South—seen through Northern eyes it is a literature filled with freaks, outcasts, characters deformed physically and spiritually. In O'Connor's fiction we get our fair share of the grotesque—an unctuous Bible salesman who steals a girl's wooden leg; a serial killer called the Misfit who slaughters a grandmother; a one-armed tramp who swindles and then abandons a deaf girl. It is easy to call this kind of literature morbid, to say that it presents an excessively, unfairly ugly world. But the world is full of fallen souls. If the rubble were cleared from our eyes, we would doubtlessly see the grotesque on Wall Street as often as we would see it in Georgia or Alabama or Texas. The grotesque is the fallenness of man made visible through distortion. As O'Connor said of her classic story "A Good Man is Hard to Find" ([1953]1971):

> This story has been called grotesque, but I prefer to call it literal. A good story is literal in the same sense that a child's drawing is literal. When a child draws, he doesn't intend to distort but to set down exactly what he sees, and as his gaze is direct, he sees the lines that create motion. Now the lines of motion that interest the writer are usually invisible. They are lines of spiritual motion.
>
> *p. 113*

This is exactly right—the child does distort when he draws, but he distorts *toward the truth*, not falsifying but presenting the spiritual in the physical. The child draws exactly what he sees, and he sees everything. For this reason, the honesty of a child can be brutal and penetrating, his drawings terrifying and revelatory. But a child's art is never moralizing.

To illustrate the mystery of looking, I will concentrate on O'Connor's story "Parker's Back" ([1965]1971) which recounts the wayward, sinful, but Christ-haunted life of a man named Parker. The story opens:

> Parker's wife was sitting on the front porch floor, snapping beans. Parker was sitting on the step, some distance away, watching her sullenly. She was plain, plain. The skin on her face was thin and drawn as tight as the skin on an onion and her eyes were gray and sharp like the point of two icepicks. Parker understood why he had married her—he couldn't have got her any other way—but he couldn't understand why he stayed with her now. She was pregnant and pregnant women were not his favorite kind. Nevertheless, he stayed as if she had him conjured. He was puzzled and ashamed of himself.
>
> *p. 510*

We learn a lot here, but mostly what we learn is that Parker is a man who does not like what he sees. The visible world pains him. Why? Because he cannot see underneath—he cannot see all that is there. All he can see is a surface that is ugly to him (the outermost layer of his wife's onion-face), and that surface does not explain his behavior, behavior that tortures him not because it is the wrong behavior but because he does not understand the reason for it. The answer to the question that haunts him (Why do I stay with this woman?) is that Parker stays because of what *he sees but does not know that he sees*, or is as yet incapable of seeing. The mystery begins already: the concrete visible world is presented (is confessed) but what is really being seen is kept hidden, its value still replete with potential energy.

O'Connor quickly puts in front of the reader the vision (the mysterious looking) around which the story and its iconography turn. She writes:

> Parker was fourteen when he saw a man in a fair, tattooed from head to foot. Except for his loins which were girded with a panther hide, the man's skin was patterned in what seemed from Parker's distance … a single intricate design of brilliant color. The man, who was small and sturdy, moved about on the platform, flexing his muscles so that the arabesque of men and beasts and flowers on his skin appeared to have a subtle motion of its own. Parker was filled with emotion, lifted up as some people are when the flag passes … . When the show was over, he had remained standing on the bench, staring where the tattooed man had been, until the tent was almost empty. Parker had never before felt the least motion of wonder in himself. Until he saw the man at the fair, it did not enter his head that there was anything out of the ordinary about the fact that he existed. Even then it did not enter his head, but a peculiar unease settled in him. It was as if a blind boy had been turned so gently in a different direction that he did not know his destination had been changed.
>
> *p. 512*

Again, there is looking, and there is mystery. Parker sees something at the fair, something mysterious and primal, and the vision redirects him every so slightly. But, as the analogy that closes the scene confirms, he is still blind despite having seen so much, despite the redirection.

What is the nature and effect of this blindness? Parker begins to cover his entire body with tattoos: arms, legs, chest, abdomen, everywhere on his body but on his back, because he can't see his back and he can see no purpose in having a tattoo that he can't see. We quickly recognize the blunder. Parker's mistake is that he believes that what he saw at the fair as a 14-year-old boy were tattoos. But that is not what he saw, not at all. He saw a mystery, something about the nature of human life and human spirituality that touched him but to which he is still essentially blind. But his tragedy is that he does not know that he saw so much, and confuses God's likeness (which he saw) with God's mystery (which he saw but did not know he saw).

Between the age of 14 and the moment he meets his wife, Parker is essentially lost, a drinker and fighter, a Navy man, an itinerant worker, all the while covering himself in ink—which it is worth noting is what a writer writes with. Upon meeting his wife, Sarah Ruth, he finds her profoundly ugly and cannot understand why he is drawn to her. While the nature of the attraction is mysterious, it clearly has something to do with her hatred for his tattoos. He tries to seduce her with them, but she insists they are a "heap of vanity" (p. 515). As her grip on him tightens, Parker becomes ever more distressed about how he sees the world.

> The view from the porch stretched off across a long incline studded with iron weed and across the highway to a vast vista of hills and one small mountain. Long views depressed Parker. You look out into space like that and you begin to feel as if someone were after you, the navy or the government or religion.
>
> *p. 516*

As we know, Parker cannot tolerate his vision of the world, not because it is shabby, but because he cannot see the world he sees—though mystery enters his eyes, he cannot see it; he cannot see what he must be able to see in order to save himself. The pain of this kind of seeing is devastating, and the only solution is the most obvious one. "Dissatisfaction began to grow so great in Parker that there was no containing it outside of a tattoo. It had to be his back" (p. 519). Not only does it have to be his back, it has to be a tattoo of a "religious subject" and be one that his wife "will not be able to resist," that will convince his wife of something very important that he wishes to convince her of.

Then, out in the field on a tractor, thinking of the design that he will get on his back, Parker suffers an accident that wakes him to God's mystery.

> As he circled the field his mind was on a suitable design for his back. The sun, the size of a golf ball, began to switch regularly from in front to behind him, but he appeared to see it both places as if he had eyes in the back of his head. All at once he saw the tree reaching out to grasp him. A ferocious thud propelled him into the air, and he heard himself yelling in an unbelievably loud voice, 'GOD ABOVE!' He landed on his back while the tractor crashed upside down into the tree and burst into flame. The first thing Parker saw were his shoes, quickly being eaten by the fire; one was caught under the tractor, the other was some distance away, burning by itself. He was not in them.
>
> *p. 521*

Parker finally sees what he had seen but not known he had seen all his life. Vision had always stood between Parker and the world around him. Now, *seeing*, the world reaches out and touches him. Whether what he sees is eternal hellfire or the intensity of the grace that the world offers to him, the reader must decide. But the effect is immediate and transformative.

> Parker did not allow himself to think on the way to the city. He only knew that there had been a great change in his life, a leap forward into a worse unknown, and that there was nothing he could do about it.
>
> *p. 521*

Here we see the full genius of Flannery O'Connor. Any lesser writer would have ended the story right there, with a full transformation. Parker would have seen at last, and seeing all, been saved. But in O'Connor's hands grace is not so easily won, and Parker, despite seeing, still is blind to some part of mystery, for he cannot see that God can forgive him—he believes that his fate is sealed, that "there was nothing he could do about it." Parker sees a "worse unknown," something that he can see and recognize and fear, but that he does not know.

A mania seizes Parker, a frantic desire to gain some control over his fate. Desperate, he once again resorts to tattoos. He visits the tattoo artist, who like all second-rate artists can only offer imagery, approximation. The artist asks Parker what tattoo he would like:

> "God," Parker said.
> "Father, Son or Spirit?"
> "Just God," Parker said impatiently. "Christ. I don't care. Just so it's God."
>
> *p. 522*

The desperation and the provincialism are at once hilarious and heartbreaking. He cannot recognize God, and the proof of this is that he trusts the artist to show him a fine one. The artist gives Parker a book of religious tattoos to look through, and after deliberating Parker chooses a "Byzantine Christ with all-demanding eyes" (p. 522). "You found what you want?" asks the artist. Parker thinks he has, though, of course, what he has found in the artist's book is not God, but an image.

The tattoo takes two days to finish. At the end of the first day, the tattoo is complete, except it has no eyes; "The eyes had yet to be put in" (p. 523). Parker spends a sleepless night in Haven of Light Christian Mission, his dreams toothed with visions of the tree that had tried to grasp him and of the flames he had seen. The following day he returns to the tattoo parlor, where God's eyes are put in. Parker does not want to look at the tattoo, but the artist, being an artist, forces Parker to look, whereupon Parker turns pale and flees. He ends up at a bar, where he chances to reveal to some of the patrons that he has a new tattoo. The men forcibly tear Parker's shirt off of him, then promptly mock him for having "got religion" (p. 526). Afterwards, shaken by the confrontation, he looks inward:

> Parker sat for a long time on the ground in the alley behind the pool hall, examining his soul. He saw it as a spider web of facts and lies that was not at all important to him but which appeared to be necessary in spite of his opinion. The eyes that were now forever on his back were eyes to be obeyed. He was as certain of it as he had ever been of anything.
>
> *p. 527*

The eyes on Parker's back are eyes that he cannot look into, and they are eyes that he cannot look through, for they are God's eyes. He still only has his own eyes. He can still only see so much. But Parker has learned the lesson O'Connor wishes us to learn, the lesson of the mystery of looking, which is that we see more than we realize, but we never see all. Put another way, literature, like religious faith, teaches us to see everything that can be seen with human eyes, to see all the sin and falleness and grace that, to so many of us, is everywhere present and nowhere visible.

The mystery of thinking

"By thinking of things you could understand them" (p. 45). So says Stephen Dedalus in *Portrait of an Artist as a Young Man* (Joyce, 1922). What Stephen's realization speaks to is not just his own awakening to the extent and powers of his own mind; it speaks to the awakening of the ape into human life. The ape who understands this is no longer an ape—like Kafka's Red Peter, he may remember his ape life, but his ape life is a life to which he cannot return. It is not simply self-consciousness that marks us as human; it is our belief that the world is something worth thinking about. If what Stephen Dedalus says is true, why is it true? Why is it that by thinking about the world we can understand it? Nobody knows, and, of course, this is the first indication that the statement may not be true. It may be the greatest lie there is.

Flannery O'Connor, and many other writers who share in her belief in the mystery of looking, would disagree with Joyce, or would think that what he says is only partly true. For O'Connor, thinking—at least as Joyce imagines thinking—is too filled with ungainly abstractions, with worship of logic, with modernism's attack on mystery and faith, to be believed wholeheartedly. Certainly, a great many people think and think but do not understand; and, perhaps, they do not understand because they think too much. I am reminded of David Foster Wallace's story "The Depressed Person" (1999), in a which a girl confuses her own obsessive thoughts with thinking, and suffers terribly for the confusion, much as certain infants eat food, regurgitate it, and swallow it again, believing they are eating when they ultimately are not, and end up dying of starvation. The girl in Wallace's story starves on her own obsessions.

But thinking is for many writers central to the mystery upon which their writing is founded. This does not mean that they believe in thinking unreservedly, that they avert their eyes from the lie that may lurk at the center of Stephen Dedalus' epiphany. To believe that about thinking would be disastrous for the writer— thinking that does not know its limitations converts all unknowns into knowns, thereby eliminating mystery and bringing the medium to an end. Rather, thinking is two-faced. On the one hand, we, like Stephen Dedalus, believe in thinking. We are human, and for us, "thought goes on" (James 1890, p. 225). We cannot let go of our love of it. On the other hand, thinking is the lie we tell ourselves so that we may sleep comfortably in what will always be mystery—reality, God, the emotions, us. We think so as not to know the truth about it all, a truth too unknowable to bear. We recall Coetzee's assertion about confession—that the mind cannot come to rest on the truth, for any truth must be subject to doubt, for doubt is the means by which we dispatch illusions and discover the deeper truths those illusions were concealing. Skepticism does not defeat thinking—it allows for thinking while drawing its limit. It allows for what thinking can discover to co-exist with what thinking cannot discover, which we call mystery. This is the two-sidedness of thinking that supplies the mystery of thinking to those writers inclined to use it.

The mystery of thinking—which, like O'Connor's mystery of looking, exists within a paradox of seeing what we do not see, of thinking what we cannot think—is central to the novels of J.M. Coetzee. Rarely do characters in Coetzee's novels see very much; but they are thinking all the time, or existing in the mystery around thinking, or succumbing to great effect to what is not thinkable. Take, as an example, Coetzee's *Life and Times of Michael K* (1985). Michael K, the protagonist, is a hare-lipped simpleton and a gardener, living in a war-torn South Africa. In Cape Town, his mother falls ill, and Michael K embarks on a journey to transport his mother—in a wheelbarrow—to the tiny Karoo town of Prince Albert, a preposterous distance to cover by foot. The novel records their journey, his mother's death, his subsistence on the land, and his imprisonment.

Michael K is a simpleton and, like all simple people, he has been told not to put too much faith in thinking. Thinking is not something he is good at; if he wishes to understand the world, he must understand it some other way. This is what it means to be a simpleton in literature—not that you are stupid, but that your best chance of understanding the world won't be by thinking about it. Thinking about the world, so the world tells the simpleton, you will get nowhere; you will not understand it; you will starve. Michael K believes this. Though he spent his "childhood in the company of other variously afflicted and unfortunate children learning the elements of reading, writing, counting, sweeping, scrubbing, bed-making, dishwashing, basketweaving, woodwork and digging" (p. 4), at 15 years old he is out of the school system for good, having taken up a job where talents other than thinking are required: the job of gardener, caretaker of nature. During his journey to Prince Albert, Michael K scarcely thinks; over time, gradually, he recedes into nature, into existence. When he does think, his thoughts are unlike most thoughts. For example, when a stranger tells Michael K, "People must help each other" (p. 48), we get the following:

> K allowed this utterance to sink into his mind. Do I believe in helping people? he wondered. He might help people, he might not help them, he did not know beforehand, anything was possible. He did not seem to have a belief, or did not seem to have a belief regarding help. Perhaps I am the stony ground, he thought.
>
> *p. 48*

Faced with the prospect of thinking, Michael K manages only the fool's wise tautologies; finally, unable to think, he resorts to an impossible thought—"Perhaps I am the stony ground." He thinks mystery, but in a way that, at this stage, is only partially profound, for his thinking is so primitive, so noncommittal, that if we let him go on thinking we would expect to find that he would eventually think he was not the stony ground, but something else. Without consequences, without anything to attach themselves to, thoughts tend to fall apart and grow absurd or idle. Michael K is very far from believing in thinking as a way of understanding himself and the world; he has no faith in thinking, but being human he goes on thinking, if only just a little.

As Michael K retreats further into the barren land, as he sleeps in caves or feeds on raw pumpkin, his thoughts more and more take on the two-sidedness of the mystery of thinking.

> So he climbed higher, zigzagging up the slope till the road through the pass disappeared from sight and he was looking over the vast plain of the Karoo, with Prince Albert itself miles below. He found a new cave and cut bushes for the floor. He thought: Now surely I have come as far as a man can come; surely no one will be mad enough to cross these plains, climb these mountains, search these rocks to find me; surely now that in all the world only I know where I am, I can think of myself as lost.
>
> *p.66*

Michael K's thoughts are more certain here than they were in the previous passage. But the truth of his statement has a doubt to equal it; his certainty is matched by mystery. For his thought is that there can be someplace so remote in the world that he can exist without thinking, or at least a place where his thinking will be unknown, and so spare that it will hardly raise him out of the continuum of existence. He will think, but not so as to understand.

> I am becoming a different kind of man, he thought, if there are two kinds of man. If I were cut, he thought, holding his wrists out, looking at his wrists, the blood would no longer gush from me but seep, and a little seeping dry and heal. I am becoming smaller and harder and drier every day. If I were to die here … I would be preserved whole, like someone in the desert drowned in sand.
>
> *p.67*

If these are thoughts, they are the thoughts of a man who does not think because he is the stony ground, or at minimum a man who is thinking himself into the mind of one whose thoughts amount quite nearly to zero. Just as Parker saw without seeing, Michael K thinks without thinking.

Michael K survives the camps and makes it back to Cape Town. There, finally, he actually thinks, in much the same way as Parker finally sees. Coetzee writes, "K tossed restlessly on the cardboard. It excited him, he found, to say, recklessly, *the truth, the truth about me. 'I am a gardener,'* he said again, aloud" (p. 182). For an instant, Michael K is not afraid to believe what he thinks. A space opens up from which doubt is momentarily absent. I am a gardener. A thought that is both as plain as plain could be, and inscrutable. What does it mean? What is the truth of this thought? The meaning we do not know, but we do not doubt the thought. The thought is a known mystery; the mystery remains mysterious while also making perfect sense. But, instantly, the clearance that had opened collapses. The very next sentence brings with it a flood of doubt: "On the other hand, was it not strange for a gardener to be sleeping in a closet within sound of the beating of the waves of the sea? I am more like an earthworm, he thought" (p. 182). The truth is picked up and carried on down the road by doubt.

Soon after, Michael K is able to think about his life from a vantage point outside of it, something that he had struggled to do before.

> The mistake I made, he thought, going back in time, was not to have had plenty of seeds, a different packet of seeds for each pocket: pumpkin seeds, marrow seeds, beans, carrot seeds, beetroot seeds, onion seeds, tomato seeds, spinach seeds. Seeds in my shoes too, and in the lining of my coat, in case of robbers along the way. Then my mistake was to plant all my seeds together in one patch. I should have planted them one at a time spread out over miles of veld in patches of soil no larger than my hand, and drawn a map and kept it with me at all times so that every night I could make a tour of the sites to water them. Because if there was one thing I discovered out in the country, it was that there is time enough for anything.
>
> p. 182

This thought is of the same nature as the previous one, but it is an eternal thought, a thought about the world and not simply about himself. It is a thought suited to Michael K, for it is finally a thought that tries to understand the world and his own place in the world—a proper human thought—as well as a thought whose basis is mystery. There is time enough for everything. Here is a thought that the novel has shown to be true, and a thought still just outside of the uncrackable shell of mystery. For Coetzee, thinking of a certain kind is linked to domination, to a mastering of nature, to the colonization of non-European countries. This kind of thinking Michael K forswears and even fears—thinking that is arrogant enough to believe without reservation that by "thinking about things we can understand them." Michael K has managed to have a thought that respects the world enough not to understand it too much, but a thought that is bold enough to mark the one who thinks it as human, and therefore willing to be human in a way that Michael K had all his life been told he was too simple to be.

The mystery of language

Among the most famous passages in all of Vladimir Nabokov's *Lolita* (1955) is the moment when Humbert Humbert first lays eyes on 12-year-old Dolores "Lolita" Haze and immediately finds her to be the second coming of the "initial girl-child" he had passionately loved as a boy. Nabokov writes:

> There came a sudden burst of greenery … from a mat in a pool of sun, half-naked, kneeling, turning about on her knees, there was my Riviera love peering at me over dark glasses. It was the same child—the same frail, honey-hued shoulders, the same silky supple bare back, the same chestnut head of hair. A polka-dotted black kerchief tied around her chest hid from my aging

ape eyes, but not from the gaze of young memory, the juvenile breasts I had fondled one immortal day. And, as if I were the fairy-tale nurse of some little princess … I recognized the tiny dark-brown mole on her side. With awe and delight … I saw again her lovely in-drawn abdomen where my southbound mouth had briefly paused; and those puerile hips on which I had kissed the crenulated imprint left by the band of her shorts.

p. 39

This passage, and many others in the novel, is filled with looking and with the incandescent details that we associate both with vision and with Nabokov's prose style. Just in this scene, we have Humbert's prurient gaze and Lolita's return gaze; that which is concealed from Humbert's "aging ape eyes"; and all that Humbert sees in his mind's eye matching up with the physical details he finds on Lolita's body. Humbert Humbert has a fantastic eye, we immediately think; he sees so much. Throughout the novel the physical detail is astonishing. In Humbert's hands a hydrant is "a hideous thing, really, painted a thick silver and red, extending the red stumps of its arms to be varnished by the rain which like stylized blood dripped upon its argent chains" (p. 106). Reading this, how can we think anything else but that Nabokov, like Flannery O'Connor, puts vision at the heart of the story he wishes to tell?

But careful attention tells a different story about Humbert Humbert. The truth is that he does not see; despite everything that he seems to see, he is perhaps the blindest character in all of 20th-century literature. Humbert does not see Dolores Haze, a seventh-grade American girl enjoying an innocent sprawl in the sunshine. If he saw that—saw her as a young human being deserving of protection and love—he could never prey on her as he does. He finds everything real about her vulgar, a threat to the solipsistic bubble of fantasy in which he lives and writes and remembers. What is really in front of Humbert is Dolores Haze; all he can ever see is Lolita. "But in my arms she was always Lolita" (p. 9).

My point is that we misunderstand *Lolita* if we imagine that Humbert Humbert values seeing in the same way that Flannery O'Connor values it. O'Connor is pledged to seeing as much as she can as truthfully as she can; Humbert dedicates himself to seeing as little as he can so that he can see what he wants to see. And what he wants to "see" is a fantasy built entirely out of language, a world that he authors in the stylized way he prefers and whose bubble cannot be pierced by empathy or morality. Thus, the endless detail of *Lolita*, the vast catalogue of nouns and adjectives. Collectively, rich and detailed descriptions lend Humbert's world the concreteness needed to convince himself, and us the readers, of its reality. But of course, almost none of it is concrete; each sentence, so deliberate and stylized and unmistakably penned, belies the truth, a truth that Humbert Humbert attempts to get out in front of by acknowledging it. He cries, "Oh, my Lolita, I have only words to play with" (p. 32). He "leaf[s] again and again through these miserable memories" (p. 13), as through pages in a book. Elsewhere, he marvels, "I am anticipating a little, but I cannot help running my memory all over the keyboard of that school year."

What Nabokov has done is to construct a world that is more concrete and particular than any world we could construct for ourselves, but a world that is always just language; a world that, as it becomes more stunning, also becomes more elaborately empty. This is the mystery of language. As the invented world grows in complexity and detail it also becomes more tenuous, more transparent, more conspicuously a made object; an empty performance. The more stylized the world becomes the less it has anything to do with the world we live in—language ceases to touch reality. A gulf opens up, with the literary object on one bank and the world as we know it on the other bank. The reality of the written world is besieged by its unreality. This is the mystery of language around which *Lolita* circles: the mystery of how the created world both convinces us of its reality and everywhere belies itself as a grand lie.

Fiction whose *modus operandi* is to play this game with language rarely can pull off the feat of deleting itself in a way that is satisfactory to the reader. Many novels—including those of Nabokov, Coetzee, and Beckett—can feel at their worst like an elaborate trick played upon the reader, a process by which the author mercilessly creates the conditions for belief and connection only to undo them. This sort of cleverness becomes tiresome, as the work seems ultimately to offer a garrulous, misleading silence.

To avoid this, the writer of such fiction must sneak in some truth, some pathos, some language that is not a fib. Frequently, the manicured illusion is dropped momentarily, and we are allowed to see or think over or past language (though, of course, it is all in the end language). Vera Nabokov, Vladimir's wife and editor, found that the accusation that *Lolita* was pornographic missed the entire point of the novel. She wrote in her diary:

> Lolita discussed by the paper from every possible point of view except one: that of its beauty and pathos. Critics prefer to looks for moral symbols, justification, condemnation, or explanation of HH's predicament … I wish, though, somebody would notice the tender description of the child's helplessness, her pathetic dependence on monstrous HH, and her heartrending courage …
>
> *Quoted in Schiff, 1999, p. 236*

Vera was partly right. There indeed are moments when the language-wall that Humbert uses to seal himself off from the world loses a brick or two, as when he finally sees the pitiful life that Lolita lives as an adult and recognizes all the innocence he stole from her. Nonetheless, I do think the novel is more artifice than substance, and that these slivers of pathos are like the breadcrumbs one might add to a soup to thicken it.

This is not to say that *Lolita*, or fiction like it, is without pathos. There is pathos, but it stems not from those moments when the protagonist's mask is cast off and he must face reality with clear eyes, but from those moments when we realize how devastatingly lonely, how unreal a life can be when it is made of language. I think of one moment in particular from *Lolita*. At the very end of the novel, Humbert Humbert is driving in his car, recovering from his tussle with the pedophile Quilty. He remarks:

> The road now stretched across open country, and it occurred to me—not by way of protest, not as a symbol, or anything like that, but merely as a novel experience—that since I had disregarded all laws of humanity, I might as well disregard the rules of traffic. So I crossed to the left side of the highway and checked the feeling, and the feeling was good. It was a pleasant diaphragmal melting, with elements of diffused tactility, all this enhanced by the thought that nothing could be nearer to the elimination of basic physical laws than deliberately driving on the wrong side of the road. In a way, it was a very spiritual itch.
>
> *p. 306*

As with everything else, Humbert sees no greater meaning in what he does—driving on the wrong side of the road is just another whim, a last perversion in a life filled with them. When Humbert says this is "merely a novel experience," he sincerely means it is a new experience. But, of course, it is a "novel experience" in another sense, in the literary sense. This is a "novel experience," the experience of a novel—Humbert wants to feel what it is like to exist inside a "real" book before that book comes to an end. This is perhaps the only time in the novel when he *feels* the unreality of his own life, the weightlessness of his own body. He notices that he has starved on language. And with panic, like one who dreams they are dead and thrashes about in a frantic effort to put the soul back into the flesh, Humbert tries to make himself real, consequential, substantive by risking himself. In risking himself, he tries to confirm the life of the body, to make sure that he is in fact there; that he did not dream himself up.

And it is this fleeting feeling of being a body with a spirit inside of it that produces the sole epiphany that Humbert comes to about his cruelty. Stopping on an embankment, the police closing in on him, Humbert hears something—a sound that carries in it all the reality he had rejected.

> What I heard was but the melody of children at play, nothing but that, and so limpid was the air that within this vapor of blended voices, majestic and minute, remote and magically near, frank and divinely enigmatic—one could hear now and then, as if released, an almost articulate spurt of vivid laughter, or the rack of a bat, or the clatter of a toy wagon, but it was all really too far for the eye to distinguish any movement in the lightly etched streets. I stood listening to that musical vibration from my lofty slope, to those flashes of separate cries with a kind of demure murmur for background, and then I knew that the hopelessly poignant thing was not Lolita's absence from my side, but the absence of her voice from that concord.
>
> *p. 308*

Final thoughts

For some time now, the world has been committed to *illumination*—to reducing the amount that is unknown and increasing the amount that is known. That is what we mean by science, and by almost every modern branch of knowledge, including the study of literature and psychoanalysis. But why must this be so? What law is there that our professions must decrease the quantity of the unknown and increase the quantity of the known? I know of no such law. What I am raising here is the possibility that psychoanalysis—like literature—is not awaiting an analyst who will reveal the truth, but an analyst who will *replenish the stores of mystery*; the analyst who can reverse course and convert the known into the unknown when such grace is called for. We are awaiting the analyst who understands about the patient what Flannery O'Connor understood about stories, which is that "the meaning of a story does not begin except at a depth where adequate motivation and adequate psychology and the various determinations have been exhausted." The analyst must understand that we suffer as much from knowing ourselves as from not knowing ourselves; that some portion of our suffering is a result of our having lost contact with mystery, not a result of living in mystery. Such an analyst, I believe, will find in literature a bottomless reserve of mystery from which he can draw, and I hope that the three mysteries I have discussed here will be of some help to him when he reads. For in reading with an ear turned to mystery the psychoanalyst puts back in as much as he takes out, allowing for the economy of writing, the economy of psychoanalysis perhaps, to carry on.

Note

1   This paper was presented as the keynote address at a conference organized by the São Paulo Psychoanalytic Society, "Dialogues in Contemporary Psychoanalysis: the Represented and Unrepresented in Psychic Life," São Paulo, Brazil, August 1–3, 2014. A Portuguese translation was published in The Represented and Unrepresented in Psychic Life (Kultura 2015). The original English version, with a revised ending, was later published in fort da: The Journal of the Northern California Society for Psychoanalytic Psychology (Ogden 2017b).

PART II
Bridging problems

2

FROM LITERATURE TO PSYCHOANALYSIS

J.M. Coetzee's foray[1]

The Good Story: Exchanges on Truth, Fiction, and Psychoanalytic Psychotherapy (2015) is a collection of email exchanges between novelist J.M. Coetzee and Arabella Kurtz, a clinical psychologist currently completing the psychotherapy training program at the Tavistock Clinic. Their correspondence, which began in 2008, concerns matters broadly relating to literature and psychoanalysis, though each narrows their respective fields considerably. Coetzee does so by turning his attention to how fictional narratives are constructed and the relationship this may have to how patients and therapists construct narratives about themselves and each other in analysis, Kurtz by generally adhering to a theoretically orthodox, primarily Freudian view of psychoanalysis.

The point of the book is, we gather, to witness how a novelist and a psychoanalyst sound and think when discussing matters of the greatest importance to both: namely, the stories human beings tell about themselves and others in an effort to describe what it is like for them (and others) to be human beings in conflict, and why and how such stories correspond with or diverge from historical or emotional truths. Coetzee, never having been in analysis himself, never having had clinical training of any kind, plays the part of curious amateur to Kurtz's wizened professional. In each of the 11 chapters of the book, Coetzee writes first, proposing questions and lines of inquiry to which Kurtz responds as psychoanalyst. *The Good Story* is, then, a tennis match in which Coetzee is always serving. This is regrettable, as it adds to an imbalance of authority already unavoidable in a discussion between a Nobel Laureate and a trainee. Though I suspect that Coetzee and Kurtz would disagree with me, their exchanges are not exploratory in spirit (as they claim in the Author's Note) but are in essence argumentative; they are having a debate. Coetzee is all along insisting upon a theory of storytelling (its goals and limits, both in fiction and analysis) that Kurtz, on behalf of psychoanalysis, rejects on the basis of its rigidity and impracticality. But her inexperience, in combination with Coetzee's seniority and clout and advantage in establishing his terms before she has had her turn, lead to a series of "returns" that tend to land short or wide. Below, I elaborate on what I think Coetzee contributes to psychoanalytic and narrative theory, and say more of what I think Kurtz wanted to say about the inner workings of psychoanalysis but couldn't, and what she ought to have said but didn't about language and its relationship to literary and psychoanalytic truth.[2]

The issue of greatest concern to Coetzee, to which he returns again and again over the course of the conversation, is as follows: Why should it matter, therapeutically, whether the story a patient tells about himself conforms to the truth? If, as we acknowledge, the past is a story we tell, and the function of the story we tell about ourselves is to help us love and work (to help us, in the Aristotelian sense, flourish), why shouldn't a therapist help the patient to land upon a story about themselves that is relatively (even entirely) unconstrained by reality (assuming that an invented story could serve the patient better than a story told in obligation to some sense of historical truth)? Might we not be happier, wonders Coetzee, if we became more creative, more inventive, more compelling fictioneers in relation to ourselves, rather than forever fretting about self-delusion? Perhaps each of us (in collusion with an analyst when needed) ought to try to learn to tell a *good* story, as opposed to a true story, about ourselves. Memory is terribly malleable, the facts about ourselves often irretrievable; an "authentic self" may be a gooey fantasy of self-realization. As such, advises Coetzee:

> It will be enough if we can settle on fictions of ourselves which we can inhabit more or less comfortably, fictions that interact sans friction with the fictions of those around us. In fact, that would be my notion of a good society, even an ideal society: one in which, for each of us, our fiction (our fantasy) of ourself goes unchallenged; and where some grand Leibnizian presiding force sees to it that all the billions of personal fictions interlock seamlessly, so that none of us need stay awake at night wondering anxiously whether the world we inhabit is real.
>
> *p. 177*

Taken seriously, this is a plan of action for creating a self-determining society, one more or less free of historical determination or guilt, and thereby free to construct itself as if nothing external constrained it. In his more recent novels and letters, for example *Diary of a Bad Year,* Coetzee has proposed similar fantasies, wherein the state and the global economy are set back to zero through collective will.[3]

Kurtz has no trouble laying out the reasons why a bottomless liberty of self-invention is neither practical nor desirable. It is true, as she says, that we are social creatures whose sense of well-being and ability to thrive are predicated on a capacity to share in the part of reality that is common, and to forge relationships based on this shared reality with those people who know us well enough to contribute to our story. Furthermore, she says, "a narrative about one's life that is too self-serving in the way you describe will have a frailty, a brittleness, a tendency to come undone on its own terms" (p. 5). When a patient's story is brittle (too brittle to be remade alone), psychoanalysis can be a space in which another story can be told, this time a story that emerges and belongs to neither the patient nor the analyst, but is their shared creation and can be both examined and reclaimed by the patient (this is my elaboration of what I believe Kurtz means by "relational truth" [p. 137] in psychoanalysis). I will return to other developments in psychoanalytic and literary thought that clarify why, from the vantage point of psychoanalysis, a patient must do more than simply tell the right story about themselves, whether we take the right story to be the "true" story or the self-serving story.

Unconvinced by Kurtz, Coetzee proposes his own, to my knowledge original, explanation for why we refuse to believe that we can supplant the past and reinvent ourselves by swiping our memories and installing new ones (p. 24). Coetzee suggests that the reason a psychoanalyst does not believe in this sort of reinvention is the same as the reason held by the fiction writer: each has a stake in maintaining a particular sense of justice that prohibits such reinvention. Coetzee believes "we should see the therapeutic dialogue as a quest for the truth before we see it as a way of making people feel good about themselves" (p. 60). There is, inherent to us all, "a longing or nostalgia for the one and only truth" (p. 68), and this longing for truth is sustained by a sense of justice. We would find it unjust to imagine that those who commit terrible crimes could simply rewrite their pasts and live happily ever after under the spell of a fiction they have chosen for themselves. In other words, the repressed *must* return because it would be unjust for it not to. The justice of the legal system can be evaded, but not a justice system that is part and parcel of the way in which the mind works. The world, we might say, has a psychobiological fairness at its core; it appears to be in the nature of truth to pursue us, in the nature of human beings to long for the truth even as we wish to leave it behind, and in the nature of consoling fictions to be exposed as lies.

What is most remarkable about this line of thought is that justice, as Coetzee understands it, is not derived from religion or divine scales, but from the justice of storytelling itself. That is, inherent to any story is a particular economy, one that cannot be broken if the story is to be a good one. In any story in which the hero attempts to deny his past and invent a different life for himself (as a patient might), the past that is denied invariably returns. As Coetzee puts it:

> One of the basic story-plots has the following shape. During his youth a man (it is usually a man) commits a shameful act, perhaps even a crime. He runs away, covers his tracks, takes a new name, makes a new life for himself in some faraway place. Years pass. He marries and has children; he becomes a pillar of the new community. He begins to allow himself to think his secret is safe, he has escaped his past. Then one day a stranger arrives in town and begins asking nosy questions. Implacably, step by step, the man's secret is uncovered. He is shamed; he is ruined.

p. 32

The fiction that the hero tries to live under is, in the end, exposed as fiction, and the past that was buried besieges him. The pattern must be that a person changes from a seeming self to a true self. "It is hard, perhaps impossible, to make a novel that is recognizably a novel out of the life of someone who is from beginning to end comfortably sustained by fictions. We make a novel only by exposing those fictions" (p. 191).[4] A story in which a man invents his own story without repercussion, without the justice of coming to terms with who he has really been, is unthinkable. From the outside looking in, it is unthinkable because it is cosmically unjust; from the inside looking about, it is unthinkable because stories do not work that way. A good story is, by this logic, just—it is not a series of ever better fictions, but fictions that are haunted by facts such that justice prevails, or at the very least rears its ugly head.

Psychoanalysis, so Coetzee's thinking goes, reproduces the economy of storytelling. The return of the repressed, defenses, projection, they are all ways of propping up a belief in the good story, which is a just story, in which progress is reflected in a movement from the seeming self to the true self. Failure to become a more authentic self, we know from literature, is a spiritual failure with emotional and physical consequences (think *Madame Bovary*). Whether the justice they see in the world is really there or is something they have invented, the psychoanalyst and the storyteller have pledged themselves to the truth born of the just order of things. Consider in this context the story of Oedipus, the archetypal psychoanalytic tale. Laius, King of Thebes, fears a prophecy that his son will be his murderer. When his wife, Jocasta, bears a son, Laius gives the infant to a shepherd to abandon on a mountainside and perish of exposure. The shepherd takes pity on the infant, and it comes to pass that the child, later to be named Oedipus, is adopted and raised by the King of Corinth and his wife. When Oedipus grows to be a man, he learns of the prophecy that he will murder his father and lie with his mother, and so (not knowing the story of his adoption) leaves Corinth in the hope of avoiding his fate. Nearing Thebes, Oedipus quarrels with, and then kills, a man in a chariot (his birth-father, Laius, whom Oedipus does not know is his father). Subsequently he solves the riddle of the Sphinx, freeing Thebes from plague, and becomes King and husband to his birth mother Jocasta. The prophecies are fulfilled. When the truth is revealed, Jocasta commits suicide; Oedipus blinds himself in anguish, then goes into exile. If we put the story in different terms, it reads as follows. A father commits a terrible act (attempted infanticide), then attempts to live life as if he did not commit such an act. The infant survives to manhood, but when informed that the story of his life will be one in which he will murder his father and marry his mother, he attempts to replace his true story with a fictional story. However, the fiction gradually comes undone; he submits to the true story, a story so unbearable that he must impose a literal blindness upon himself as a substitute for the figurative blindness that was the consoling, fictive life he had once led. In the end, so says the storyteller, Oedipus's true self supplants the fictional self he had hoped to invent because the grammar of stories forbids a different ending. In the end, says the psychoanalyst, the lesson is that the repressed returns to conscious self-awareness;

no amount of conscious effort or will can eclipse our past, can bury those parts of ourselves that make us who we are.

Coetzee regards such interpretations as persuasive but self-serving fictions. Consequently, he proposes a different reading, which to my mind is the premise of his contribution to psychoanalytic theory. About the story of Oedipus, he asks:

> But what if the true secret, the inadmissible secret, the secret about secrets, is that secrets can indeed be buried and we can indeed live happily ever after? What if this big secret is what the Oedipus story is trying to bury? In other words, what if our culture, perhaps even human culture in general, has created a form of narrative which is on the surface about the unburiability of secrets but under the surface seeks to bury the one secret it cannot countenance: that secrets can be buried, that the past can be obliterated, that justice does not reign?
>
> *p. 34*

What if, I'll add, the story of Oedipus is a myth about our human need for justice, carried in the deep structure of stories and in the even deeper structure of the human mind? Taken as an allegory of psychic life, the psychoanalytic reading of Oedipus reflects a larger faith (hope) that the justice of stories is a reflection of the justice of psychological life itself. The justice of the story of Oedipus is an expression of a justice inherent to the makeup of the mind. The mind is a just place; it is ordered for fairness. Thus, we raise defenses against replacing the true story with the invented story (the just story with the unjust story). We do not wish to imagine that stories could operate on an economy different from the economy of psychology, or that stories reflect a human (psychological) wish for justice that has no basis in reality.

Coetzee here considers whether the mind, the function of which is to make meaning, is in-built to make meaning in a way that retains a sense of justice. The mind makes meaning by forming narratives that have a just grammar to them, and operates so as to retain a sense of justice without which meaning could not be constructed. The repressed returns because, metapsychologically, unreturned repression is *a trauma* to the just economy of the mind. So, our stories, to have a therapeutic function, must be good and just. The story of Oedipus is thereby a *living out* of the healthy functioning of the mind (and of the mind's storytelling function) as it metabolizes the trauma to its meaning-making function and recalibrates to a state of cosmic, psychological, and narrative justice. It is not the truth, then, that avenges itself upon Oedipus, but the mind's justice-making function as it seeks to bury the "secret about secrets" that is its deepest truth, a truth that is sent into exile (utterly disconnected from the rest of our knowledge).

Putting aside all the objections one might raise against the motivations Coetzee attributes to psychoanalysis, his speculation—that the psychoanalytic model of mind is rooted in a heretofore unacknowledged belief that the mind is structured for justice—has implications that are far-reaching and deserve to be taken seriously. Much as Freud, in *Civilization and its Discontents* (1930), sees social organization and religious feeling as adult expressions of structures of mind developed in early childhood, Coetzee follows a line of thinking in which meaning and justice are the measures of equilibrium in a properly functioning mind. From this, one could go so far as to see other cultural and artistic institutions as generated by the operations of the human psyche: a range of religious establishments and spiritual beliefs, rules of law and government, post-religious ethics, all might carry in them a psychological need to find in human affairs a just grammar.

Specifically, Coetzee's model of mind could address matters of the greatest importance to the hermeneutics of literary interpretation. For instance, about literary criticism, we can ask: why is it that a work of literature cannot mean whatever we would like it to mean? More precisely, why are we (through our various institutions and professional degrees, our many classes on critical analysis and aesthetic appreciation) so invested in holding up objective standards for interpretation? Certainly literary criticism is founded upon the premise that not all interpretations of a work are valid. One could argue that this is due to formal aspects of the work and their plausible associations, or upon the cultural and historical contexts within which the work could reasonably be understood. In "Can We Say Absolutely Anything We Like?" (1985), Frank Kermode takes up this very question, concluding that the answer depends on whether you are inside or outside those institutions that have a vested interest in maintaining aesthetic standards: "The real difference between the outside and the inside is marked by the insistence of the outsider that he can say what he likes about Shakespeare and the tacit knowledge of the institution, which he therefore hates, that nothing he says is worth attending to" (p. 160). But the mystery is *why* we care so much about upholding standards of any kind, why so much of the educational system is dead-set on disabusing students of anything that resembles the belief that "poetry means whatever we think it means," and why, among the adult ranks, so few hold fast to anything like this belief.

The answer may be that it is a matter of the justice-meaning-making function of the mind. It is unjust for works to mean whatever we would like them to mean, for to find objective meaning in art is to support a notion of justice (i.e. one interpretation is better than another when it is supported by a form of thinking that can be acquired only through prolonged effort). Institutions that grant degrees in interpreting art protect this justice. This may be why even those ignorant of art or literature so often give up on the belief, returning to Kermode, that they can say absolutely anything. They do this not because they have been convinced otherwise, but out of a human need for justice and meaning to coincide, or in concession to a human need that they recognize and see no way to resist. Faced with opposing interpretations, the subjective view must stand down, for it is based on "nothing" and so is unjust. This may count as a great loss, believes Coetzee. Society moderates the storytelling function at its peril; it may be that the invented interpretation should stand side by side with the interpretation grown to the stem of truth.

Clearly, for Coetzee, psychoanalysis is a highly narrativized art form. Psychoanalysis believes in the truth (the true story), and in the psychological and emotional rewards of arriving at the truth. To tell the true story of oneself is to be unburdened; to tell more lies (to pass off lies as truth) is to be suspended in agony. While this will strike most as an utterly incomplete conception of psychoanalysis (as it does Kurtz), one must keep in mind that psychoanalysis is for Coetzee very closely tied to the tradition of religious confession and to the genre of confessional literature. These are subjects to which Coetzee has devoted hundreds of pages over the last 35 years, and to which he returns (through a discussion of Dostoevsky) in *The Good Story*. In both confession and psychoanalysis, so argues Coetzee in his studies of the confessional form, a person wishes to tell the whole truth about himself, and to tell this truth to someone who can grant the wholly bared story an exculpatory, and spiritually and emotionally freeing, grace. In other words, the patient, the confessor, will ideally have the listener he wants, one who can identify the truth among any fictions and grant the truth, once spoken, its power to heal.

That any such truth can be arrived at in confession, however, is subject to much doubt. In Coetzee's many non-fiction analyses and fictional illustrations of confession, the same philosophical problem arises again and again: can the self ever really tell the "essential truth" about itself without lying, or without passing off a lie as the truth? Can confession ever arrive at the truth it must finally arrive at in order to achieve moral closure, or is there "always a further level of self-understanding to be explored" (p. 41)? Surely, as Coetzee points out, any truth must be subjected to doubt, for otherwise self-deluding fictions would be passed off and inevitably accepted as truth. It is only through painstaking skepticism and a rigorous investigation of human motivation (of the sort conducted so brilliantly by Dostoevsky in such works as *Demons* [[1872]1994] and *The Idiot* [[1868]2003]) that the "real" truth can be unearthed. However, if the process of doubt has no certain resting place then there can be no final truth, only a regression to infinity. It is on this basis that Coetzee, in his novel *Disgrace*, parodies the South African Truth and Reconciliation Commission for its unsupportable notion that it can determine whether a confessant is in fact telling the truth.[5] It is on the same basis that, in *Waiting for the Barbarians* (1980), the Empire's torturer explains his interrogation method as a means of penetrating a nearly uncrackable shell of lies: "First, I get lies, you see—this is what happens—first lies, then pressure, then more lies, then more pressure, then the break, then more pressure, then the truth. That is how you get the truth" (p. 5). The torturer is here a priest, or a guide that cleaves through self-serving fictions to arrive at a truth that will bring the period of pain to an end. To the extent that it can fairly be called political, Coetzee's exhortation to abandon the truth (to live as outlaw in a truth-beholden world) is an endorsement of creative self-invention as an aspect of a politically liberated life.

It is, then, in the context of the confessional form that Coetzee's narratival and metaphysical conception of psychoanalysis must be understood. If we hold to the narrative framework of confession, in which a clear distinction is drawn between a lie and a truth (there being no third choice, such as the intersubjective alternative proposed by Kurtz, or field-theory), then Coetzee gives a fair diagram of psychoanalysis and its narrative machinery. However, where Coetzee goes too far is in presuming that a narrative logic can be used to attribute to psychoanalysis a narratively based therapeutic function. Coetzee, as I understand him, imagines the following: the psychoanalytic dialogue is a process by which a patient develops a story about himself and in which analyst and patient together determine whether it is optimal for the patient to try to tell the true story of himself or to tell an invented story about himself that would suit him better. Therefore, psychological health is a matter of arriving at a clear and beneficent narrative about oneself; this is the case whether one is "truth-directed" (Coetzee, 1992, p. 261) or fiction-directed in the storytelling process.

But of course, this is accurate only if psychoanalysis is *just* its schematic structure, and only if other aspects of psychoanalysis can in no way complicate or work beyond the bounds of the narrative schema. And the first indication that the narrative portrait Coetzee paints is unsatisfactory is that, for patients and non-patients alike, it is very possible to tell and know the truth about oneself, to have arrived at a story that in its facts and connections is indeed the right story, but still be miles from emotional or psychological health. Narrative truth, akin to confessional truth, is not enough on its own. Putting a past event into a meaningful context within a comprehensive self-narrative is but one way in which an event can become true, and but one way in which an event must be processed by the mind for the event to be synthesized into the psychological economy in a way that promotes psychological growth.

Here, in response to Coetzee's structural portrayal of psychoanalysis, I will introduce a term of psychoanalytic theory that Kurtz does not raise, but which speaks to a dimension of psychoanalysis that Kurtz rightly insists upon: "What is missing [from Coetzee's description of psychoanalysis] is a sense of us as living beings in the world: in this description it is as if we either exist only in our mind or, in some sense, not at all. External and internal experience are in combat, not in relation" (p. 16). In adding to Kurtz's rebuttal, I intend to show what else psychoanalysis must be besides narrative, and to demonstrate how Coetzee's understanding of confession and the literary narrative could be developed if he took seriously the experiential, non-narrative aspects of psychoanalysis.

Nachträglichkeit is a term—rendered in English as deferred action, in French as après-coup—used by Freud to describe a particular aspect of "psychical temporality and causality" (Laplanche and Pontalis, 1973, p. 111), specifically the way in which "experiences, impressions and memory-traces may be revised at a later date to fit in with fresh experiences and the attainment of a new stage of development." Though it is not a term that Freud ever explicitly defined or made the subject of a paper, there is little doubt it was part of his "conceptual equipment" (Laplanche and Pontalis, p. 111) as it appears again and again in his work, first in 1896 in a letter to Fliess and more than two decades later in the "Wolf Man" case (Freud, 1918), there in connection with seduction theory.[6] As Freud never embalmed the term *Nachträglichkeit* in a fixed meaning, each of us has the pleasure of understanding the term in relation to the experience of seeing Freud work with the term. In this sense, for Freud and for us, the term is always in the present, to be dealt with as something we are fortunate enough to build because it was never quite built for us.

When I build the term up in my mind in preparation for using it, I understand it in two senses: a narrative and an extra-narrative sense. The narrative sense, which was introduced by Freud, holds that something may be "deposited" in the mind that is revived later through retroactive interpretation, analysis, and re-envisioning, though the causal–temporal relation between the deposit and the revival is not altogether exact. Is the deposit a memory trace (perhaps of a trauma) already invested with pathogenic force (a "ticking time-bomb") whose activation is deferred to a later moment, or is the deposit pathogenically neutral until such time as it becomes retroactively invested with pathogenic force by the combination of the nature of the deposit itself and the new circumstances? This creates a complementarity much like the one Coetzee proposes: life unfolds linearly and at the same time is constructed retroactively (in the form of narratives we create of our past). It is only emphasis, then, that separates Freud from Coetzee: Freud most often holds to a linear causality that draws a limit on what can be retroactively invented, while Coetzee supposes that causality can be recreated in the fictional narratives we make up for ourselves.

However, there is no reason to restrict the concept of deferred action to perceptions that have been repressed as trauma. It can very well apply to events that are perceived, *remembered*, and yet pass unexperienced. In keeping this possibility afloat, we retain a fairly good reason for believing that the term troubled Freud precisely because it expressed more than an underlying ambivalence about linear and retroactive temporality—more than the various causalities that can order the narrative of human life. In fact, *Nachträglichkeit* pestered him as a concept because its greatest implication still remained to be explored even after the central ambiguity between linear-deterministic and retroactive temporality had theoretically resolved itself. The difficulty of the term may not lie solely in its "bidirectionality" (Civitarese, 2013, p. 103), but in a lurking sense that the term fails to cohere unambiguously because it contains its own limits, gesturing as it does to something extra-narrative.

The specific sense in which I understand *Nachträglichkeit* is as a term used by Freud to describe what cannot be contained in a purely narrative understanding of human life—it is the extra-narrative dimension of human experience. That is, it points our attention to what is left out of a story even when the whole story has been told. It is a term that acknowledges something that happened to us in the past but that we did not experience at the time, and the process by which we come to experience for the first time an event in the past at which we had not been able to be emotionally present. An example of this can be found in Freud's discussion of the case of the Wolf Man, who at the age of one and a half witnessed his parents having intercourse, but who, as he was not yet at a stage of sexual development that would allow him to incorporate (attribute meaning to) his perception, would only experience what he had witnessed as a dream at the age of four.[7] It is what a person who has told the entire story of themselves—who has confessed the truth to standards that would satisfy a priest—has yet to do, and must do if he is to get the relief or grace he had sought from making confession. Understood in this way, the primary challenge is in coming to recognize that the narrative (the confession) was already seemingly complete, but the experience of the narrative incomplete (and consequently not possible to include in his confession). Kurtz touches upon extreme, black-and-white separations of this sort in relation to the concept of splitting and Klein's paranoid-schizoid position. Another, more modern, conception of this phenomenon that she does not mention appears in Winnicott's paper "Fear of Breakdown" (1974), in which he states that a breakdown that a patient fears will occur has in fact already occurred in the form of a breakdown of the patient's early relationship with his mother.

A great deal is lost from both literature and psychoanalysis if we do not see that what both offer is a form of movement from the first to the second sense of deferred action—from telling a life to living it out. Confession, whether in literature or analysis, can only be brought to completion when this bridge has been crossed. This is what psychoanalysis and literature share: an *insistence* that this traversal is possible; no real kind of reading or analysis can begin until this insistence is communicated, and usually this insistence is communicated through the living out of it. Perhaps this is also what literature and psychoanalysis share: an unbreakable will to insist upon a difference between telling and more-than-telling, no matter the form this difference may take. The granite strength of this insistence—writ in the great many enactments of it—is a kind of illustrious non-negotiable, and could form the basis of a better dialogue between psychoanalysis and literature than the tremendously learned but rather wooden one we get from Kurtz and Coetzee.

Deferred action, because it contains both the narrative and the extra-narrative (experiential) dimension of confession, both reiterates Coetzee's viewpoint and adds something critical to it. It gives us a way of looking both at what must happen in confession for grace to be achieved (over and above what Coetzee recognizes), and at how literature and psychoanalysis expand upon, and expand beyond, the narrative operations that Coetzee grants under the umbrella of confession.

To illustrate this, let us look at "Stavrogin's Confession," a chapter from Dostoevsky's political novel *Demons* ([1872]1994), which was suppressed by Dostoevsky's editor for its scandalizing content, revised by Dostoevsky in an effort to have the chapter pass censorship, then eventually abandoned. This episode from *Demons* has long been important to Coetzee, as it plays a decisive part in Coetzee's depiction of Dostoevsky in *The Master of Petersburg* (1994), and is also among the select texts that Coetzee discusses in his major essay on confession, "Confession and Double Thought: Tolstoy, Rousseau, Dostoevsky" ([1985]1992). In *The Good Story*, Coetzee returns to this chapter as an illustration of the narrative mechanics of confession. In *Demons*, Nikolai Stavrogin, son of the affluent widow Varvara Petrovna, is an attractive young gentleman who, by the age of 25, has already fought several duels, and thenceforth engages in odd and destructive acts, including leading an old man around by the nose and biting a governor's ear; he is also a great seducer and destroyer of women. Above all, he suffers from indifference (a spiritual variation of the nihilism that takes political and philosophic forms in the novel), which is only alleviated for brief moments by a perverse pleasure taken in acts of brutality. The nature of Stavrogin's condition as it worsens is among the major concerns of the novel.

In the suppressed chapter, Stavrogin leaves his room following a sleepless night and proceeds to wander the streets in a directionless way until he reaches a monastery at the edge of town. He asks to see the retired Bishop Tikhon, and is promptly led to his chambers. Once they have sat down together, Stavrogin tells Bishop Tikhon of how he is "subject, especially at night, to hallucinations of a sort; how he sometimes saw or felt near him some malicious being, scoffing and 'reasonable,' 'in various faces and characters, but one and the same'" (p. 686).

After making these revelations Stravrogin quickly distances himself from them, insists he must simply see a doctor, and asserts about this demon, "It's all rubbish, terrible rubbish. It's I myself in various aspects and nothing more" (p. 686). But it is clear that Stavrogin is at a loss to make sense of what troubles him, and he and Tikhon discuss this matter until, quite abruptly, Stavrogin draws some "printed pages" (p. 690) from his pocket. He tells Tikhon that the pages are intended for publication and that nothing will stop him from publishing these pages, and demands that Tikhon read them. Tikhon does so, and we discover that they are Stavrogin's eponymous confession, in which he tells of seducing a 12-year-old girl, and then standing idly by as she enters a closet and hangs herself in shame.

In the confession, which runs for several pages, Stavrogin declares again and again that he intends to "tell everything in the firmest words, so that nothing remains hidden any longer" (p. 692). He says also: "I am setting this down precisely in order to prove the extent of my power over my memories, and how unfeeling for them I had become. I would reject them all in a mass, and the whole mass would obediently disappear each time the moment I wanted it to" (p. 702). The entire confession is told in this manner, with a veneer of cool and exacting objectivity. The remainder of the chapter is devoted to Tikhon's response to this confession; to his attempt to discuss with Stavrogin some of the motivations he might have for publishing such a confession; and to what Stavrogin may be able to do for his spiritual condition in the wake of such a revelation.

So Stavrogin has come to Tikhon with a confession, but as to what he really wants from Tikhon, and as to what Tikhon can plausibly give him, we have few clear answers. It is as if Stavrogin, in presenting his confession, is saying to Tikhon, "Here is everything that has happened, but beyond that, what do I do?" Stavrogin is not asking for forgiveness so much as asking how to move from the narrative to the extra-narrative—he is asking for the literary, for the psychoanalytic. Of course, Stavrogin does not know that is what he is asking for; he only half knows why he has come and can only foresee a purely narrative outcome, whereby his account is published and he does penance through public humiliation. Stavrogin's predicament is clear: his account perhaps satisfies the bare conditions of confession, but it does not satisfy himself, could not possibly satisfy a discerning reader, and grants none of the relief or insight that confessants seek.

Why is it that Stavrogin's confession, assiduous and detailed in so many ways, has done so little for him? There are a number of reasons, but among the most important, and the most easily overlooked, is that the terrible deed to which Stavrogin confesses is one that he has yet to in fact experience. Throughout the affair with the girl, Stavrogin suffers from an unbearable indifference that takes him out of life. His description of the seduction itself makes this clear:

> Her whole face flushed with shame. I kept whispering something to her. Finally, there suddenly occurred an odd thing, which I will never forget and which caused me some astonishment: the girl threw her arms around my neck and suddenly began kissing me terribly. Her face expressed complete admiration. I almost got up and left—so unpleasant was it in such a tiny child—out of pity. But I overcame the sudden sensation of my fear and stayed. When it was all over, she was embarrassed.
>
> *p. 696*

From Stavrogin's description of the sin, the sin itself has vanished. All he found himself capable of experiencing was the girl's admiration, which in its utter desperation becomes almost a confirmation of the perversity of life that Stravrogin is proving through his actions. A similar elision appears when the girl, in a state of despair, takes the first steps in her suicide:

> Soon I heard her hurrying steps again, she walked out the door onto the wooden gallery, from which a stairway went down, and I at once ran to my door, opened it a bit, and had just time to spy Matryosha going into a tiny shed, like a chicken coop, next to the other place. A strange thought flashed in my mind. I closed the door and—back to the window. Of course, it was impossible to believe a fleeting thought; "and yet …" (I remember everything.)
>
> *p. 699*

Stavrogin "remembers everything," and what he remembers includes a swelling conviction that the girl is going to harm herself, but the reality of the deed itself and his role in the execution of the deed are treated as mere thoughts (impersonal information) about the possibility of the deed. The event of Matryosha's suicide is filled with motion and weight and materiality ("hurrying steps," "a stairway," "wooden gallery," "a tiny shed," "a chicken coop," which is "next to the other place"). Stavrogin has only flashes of thought, as he peers emptily through a window while he waits for the girl to do what she will, "and began watching a tiny red spider on a geranium leaf, and became oblivious. I remember everything to the last moment" (p. 699).

Eventually, when enough time has passed for the girl to have harmed herself, Stavrogin learns what became of her:

> Finally, I quietly opened the door, locked it with my key, and went to the shed. The door was closed, but not locked; I knew it could not be locked, yet

I did not want to open it, but got up on tiptoe and began looking through the crack. At that very moment, as I was getting up on tiptoe, I recalled that when I was sitting by the window looking at the little red spider and became oblivious, I was thinking of how I would get up on tiptoe and reach that crack with my eyes. By putting in this trifle here, I want to prove with certainty to what degree of clarity I was in possession of my mental faculties. I looked through that crack for a long time, it was dark inside, but not totally. At last I made out what I needed … I wanted to be totally sure.

p. 700

Stravrogin's removal from life is so severe, we now learn, that he is incapable even of experiencing his own obliviousness. For even as he was oblivious, he was thinking about what he imagined he would soon be doing. And then, when the anticipated moment comes, he is thinking about how he had been thinking earlier about what he is at the moment doing. Stavrogin remembers everything, but that is because his whole life is nothing more than a story that he tells about himself, but that he cannot live. As such, all of what he ought to experience becomes mere fodder for what can be included in his memories, and can thereby be included in his confession. He stares at the dead girl for a long time not out of horror or compassion, not even to live out in any way the destruction he has caused, but to get what he "needed," which is to be sure of the facts that he will have to remember and to confess. Stavrogin's life *is* a confession, understood in the most hollow, most strictly narrative sense. Such is the extent of his indifference.

Tikhon, the reader feels from the first moment he appears, is a man of extraordinary wisdom and sensitivity. One of the great interests of reading the chapter is discovering what Tikhon will do to help Stavrogin. How will this ascetic priest respond to this confession? Here is what Tikhon does immediately after reading the confession:

Tikhon removed his glasses and began first, somewhat cautiously.
"And might it be possible to make some corrections in this document?"
"What for? I wrote it sincerely," replied Stavrogin.
"To touch up the style a little."

p. 705

Of all the ways that Tikhon might have begun to counsel Stavrogin, this may be the most unexpected. Tikhon suggests an improvement in the writing style. He begins with language, with form. The response is so miraculous and unexpected that there is no way that Stavrogin could have anticipated it. As such, the meeting between them is something that Stavrogin must experience, along with Tikhon, if he is to be helped. But the experience is to be had in art, guided by Tikhon. This is the process that the chapter describes: life is re-presented in the form of language (Stavrogin's confession) so that the artlessness of the language can be "treated" (changed into art with Tikhon's help) as a means of experiencing the life differently. Stavrogin has bared himself, but his style—its falseness—betrays him, and it is to some degree in his style that he will have to begin to live. Another way of putting it: you were not entirely present for the terrible act you committed, and that absence *numbs* the events of the life; numbing is the absence of literary style, which invests recounted events with their power to move. This confession is no more than a story—it is not yet life. As you were not there for the event, your lack of style (which is a way of thinking and feeling that invests stories with life) betrays the fact that your confession is devoid of art, which is, as George Eliot said, the nearest thing to life.[8]

The process by which Tikhon may help give to Stavrogin's confession elements of the extra-narrative that will allow Stravrogin to truly confess (to live what he confesses) is, to my mind, psychoanalytic work. It is psychoanalytic in that it will take what was dead language describing an unlived life and turn it through style (through dialogues about how best to talk) into a lived life that can be *confessed to the point of becoming art*, which is the nearest thing to life. Only life itself is complete. Confession, elevated to the level of art through style, can thereby reach the only completion of which it is really capable—an artistic completion internal to itself and in relation to the life it recreates. In this sense, literature has undergone the transformation (in countless ways) that psychoanalysis wishes to effect, and so literature becomes an archive of successful therapy. But for literature to be such an archive one must be a reader who possesses something like Tikhon's discerning; one cannot make the mistake, returning again to Kermode, of thinking that literature can mean whatever we would like it to mean. Here, then, is the real justice of literature—it gives mere stories to those who read poorly, and art to those who read well. Tikhon, faced with telling, insists upon more-than-telling, and further insists upon more-than-telling that can happen in language. In finding a way of writing that is also a way of living, so Tikhon believes, Stavrogin can now begin to confess.

Notes

1 This is a review of *The Good Story: Exchanges on Truth, Fiction and Psychoanalytic Psychotherapy* (Coetzee and Kurtz 2015). The review was previously published, in English, in the journal of the Italian Psychoanalytic Society, *Rivista di Psicoanalisi* (2016).
2 *The Good Story*, in putting literature and psychoanalysis into conversation with one another, resembles the book that I co-authored with Thomas H. Ogden, *The Analyst's Ear and the Critic's Eye: Rethinking Psychoanalysis and Literature* (2013). For this review I have drawn on ideas developed in *The Analyst's Ear* in responding to the dialogue between Coetzee and Kurtz.
3 For Coetzee's discussion of global finance, see *Here and Now* (2013), his correspondence with Paul Auster (beginning p. 28). And for my discussion of the importance of state formation to Coetzee's understanding of literature, see my article "The Coming into Being of Literature" (Ogden 2010).
4 One certainly could make the case that it is easy to envision a novel in which the hero is "sustained by fictions" all the way through. No law forbids such a novel. But, to Coetzee's point, a novel that took such a form could only be read as an ironic departure from the archetypal story-form, much as a romance that concludes with all parties bitter and lovelorn must be read as a tongue-in-cheek deviation from the original type. Further, as

Coetzee points out, one cannot have a story in which the secret is utterly buried because, in the end, "the secret is not really buried, since the reader knows it" (p. 33).

5 See my article "Reconcile, Reconciled: A New Reading of Reconciliation in J.M. Coetzee's *Disgrace*" (2012a).

6 For a review of the term, particularly in relation to contemporary theories of neurobiology, see Civitarese (2013).

7 In a footnote, Freud writes: "I mean that he understood it at the time of the dream when he was four years old, not at the time of the observation. He received the impressions when he was one and a half; his understanding of them was deferred, but became possible at the time of the dream owing to his development, his sexual excitations, and his sexual researches" (1918, p. 37).

8 From "The Natural History of German Life" (Eliot, 1990, p. 108).

3

FROM PSYCHOANALYSIS TO LITERATURE

Bion and the apes[1]

Tenerife is the largest of Spain's Canary Islands. It sits fewer than two hundred miles off the coast of West Africa, nearest Morocco. In 1912, at the behest of the neurophysicist Max Rothman, the Prussian Academy of Sciences agreed to establish the Anthropoid Station for the study of the thinking capacity of apes on the island. Rothman, in a paper outlining the conditions that would need to be met for the creation of such a station, proposed Tenerife because it "can be reached in six days from Europe; African anthropomorphs can be transported there without issue straight from Cameroun. Asian anthropomorphs can be transported there fairly easily via Tangier, where large German steamships dock en route to Asia" (Qtd. Ruiz and Sanchez 2014, p. 3). By January the following year, the first director of the project, Eugene Teuber, had arrived on the island, tasked with getting the station up and running. Teuber was not yet 24 years old and still working toward a doctorate, so he agreed only to a one-year position.

Working quickly, Teuber leased an estate on which he and his wife could live and constructed the necessary living quarters for seven chimpanzees and the "playground" on which experiments could be conducted. The playground extended for one thousand square meters, and was enclosed on all sides (including the roof) by wire mesh, which hung from a five-meter-high support pole in the center of the yard. Inside the enclosure were a few banana trees, shrubs, a jungle gym. Before his one-year term was complete, Teuber used the complex to conduct experiments into the gestural language of chimpanzees as progenitor to human language.

It was not, however, until the arrival of Teuber's successor, the psychologist Wolfgang Köhler, in December 1913 that Tenerife would become the unlikely setting for one of the most important, arguably the most ruthless, studies to have been conducted on the nature of, and conditions, for thinking. These studies, conducted from 1913 to 1917, are described in Köhler's monograph *The Mentality of*

Apes (1925), one of those rare books that is both little known and a classic. Köhler would later become one of the principal elaborators of Gestalt psychology, and several Gestalt tenets already underlie the experiments on Tenerife, namely that perception of a whole is required for intelligence; that the whole is different from the elemental parts; and that stimulus-response theories of behavior are imperfect (simian intelligent behavior was not merely a matter of trial-and-error learning, as the psychologist Edward Thorndike had proposed).

The goal of Köhler's research was, in his words, to establish "whether [animals] do not behave with intelligence and insight under conditions which require such behavior" (p. 1). To determine if apes could exhibit evidence of thinking, Köhler devised a series of experiments that shared a basic pattern: an ape would be faced with a situation that had a visible objective (a piece of fruit, usually); however, in each case "the direct path to the objective is blocked, but a roundabout way left open" (p. 4). Example: the male chimpanzee Sultan is led into the yard. Surveying the entirety of his environment, Sultan sees that from the wire mesh ceiling of the yard hangs a bunch of bananas; an out-of-reach prize. Into the yard comes Dr. Köhler, dragging behind him three wooden boxes, which he drops at different places in the yard. Köhler then leaves the yard, but continues to watch from somewhere outside the compound.

So: the man who feeds me unaccountably stopped feeding me; now my food is clearly hanging up there, where it has never hung before; there are now boxes at my disposal that were not available previously; the Man remains close by, watching me with great interest. The experiment has begun. Maybe, so has thinking.

Consider this description of Sultan's state of mind: "Sultan knows: Now one is supposed to think. That is what the bananas up there are about. The bananas are there to make one think, to spur one to the limits of one's thinking. But what must one think?" (p. 72). This is Elizabeth Costello, the eponymous character of J.M. Coetzee's quasi-novel *Elizabeth Costello* (2004). She is delivering a lecture on "The Lives of Animals." For Costello, and in this case I believe for Coetzee too, thinking emerges in response to a circumstance in which thinking is plainly expected—in which an environment is animated to make one think. Thinking is, first and foremost, a response to the pressure of the special arrangement of the environment, which supplies the desire and the frustration of the desire. However, in Coetzee's rendering, more is required than desire and frustration for thought to come into being. The environment must additionally invest in us a feeling of "supposed to." This feeling of "supposed to" leads to a recognition that there is someone or something that wishes for us to think. "That is what the bananas up there are about." They are about some wish the world, and the world's designer, has for us to think. Just as beauty would like for us to look and to continue looking (to stare), the world wants us to think about it. How does the world, and its designer, convey to us that it would like us to think? By presenting the world to us in the form of *a problem*, the solution to which is the answer to the question: "But what must one think?" The world is designed not for our general contemplation, but to draw out of us the solutions to the problems it poses. The world calls to us as a problem to be solved.

In *Learning From Experience* (1962a) and "Theory of Thinking" (1962b), Bion's conception of thinking is similar in several ways to Coetzee's conception of thinking. For Bion, thoughts exert a pressure, which is experienced as the pain of the feeling of "supposed to think." In response to the problem of this pressure, thinking develops. Most importantly for my purposes, which will eventually be to consider his experimental work of fiction *A Memoir of the Future* (1991), Bion conceives of thinking as the outcome of the demand we feel the world places on us to think the correct thought, to provide a solution to the emotional problem it poses. Thinking, for Bion, is the product of the problem posed by thoughts. That Bion formulates thinking as a problem is everywhere in the language of *Learning From Experience*: "Envy aroused by a breast that provides love, understanding, experience and wisdom poses a problem that is solved by destruction of alpha-function" (p. 11); "The theory of functions offered a prospect of solving this problem by assuming that I contained unknown functions of his personality" (p. 21); "But the problem stimulates the thought …"(p. 63); "the model is then found to be insufficiently similar to clarify the problem for which the solution is sought" (p. 80). The word "problem" appears at least thirty times in the slim book.

Attached to these problems we find the same pressures and feelings as Coetzee finds in Köhler's experiment: a feeling of "supposed to"; an environment that exerts a pressure that "require[s] an apparatus to cope" (Bion 1962b, p. 306) with it; a sense of design inherent in the environment (the environment is designed as a persecutory or pleasure-giving object); a sense that the design of the environment is one of a problem to be solved by thought. These are the conditions for the coming into being of thinking.

For both Coetzee and Bion, thinking can develop only when one is placed into a situation that one experiences as a problem; when one knows one is supposed to think; when one knows the world has been arranged "to spur one to the limits of one's thinking." Coetzee, however, goes further than Bion in that he links the conditions for the coming into being of thinking with the conditions for the coming into being of literature. Consider how the opening of *Elizabeth Costello* puts into conversation the problem of thinking and the problem of literature:

> There is first of all the problem of the opening, namely, how to get us from where we are, which is, as yet, nowhere, to the far bank. It is a simple bridging problem, a problem of knocking together a bridge. People solve such problems every day. They solve them, and having solved them push on. Let us assume that, however it may have been done, it is done. Let us take it that the bridge is built and crossed, that we can put it out of our mind. We have left behind the territory in which we were. We are in the far territory, where we want to be.
>
> *p. 1*

For Coetzee, literature comes into being much as thinking does. Upon opening a book, one finds oneself in a world that resembles reality (it is familiar) but also feels to us designed to provoke thinking (it is unfamiliarly provocative). One is faced with a problem posed by the book, a problem that exerts a pressure.

We could say that the reader is like Sultan, the author like Köhler, and the text (particularly those aspects of it that seem to call out for interpretation) like the boxes and the bananas hung out of reach. Much as Sultan must learn to build a bridge from the ground to the bananas by stacking the boxes, we must learn to build our bridge into the "far territory" wherein we have left behind the non-literary and accepted the conditions for literary experience.

Depending on whether we are reader, or text, or author, we will play a different part in the mysterious bridging problem. However, despite the different roles each may play, all are interested in a solution to the problem presented by the work. The solution will take the form of an ability to read the work so that reading becomes a process of experiencing and working out a solution to the language and life of the work. There are, then, two kinds of reading: reading that is simply the passive comprehension of language (reading without thinking), and reading of a higher order that would be akin to what Bion means by "learning from experience." A pre-conception (an instinct for reading, as well as problem solving) is mated with its frustration (how does one read at a level at which the problem of reading is solved?) to create thinking, which may involve not only interpretation but also a tolerance for the frustrations of difficult literature. This is all to say that Bion's theory of thinking also says something about reading—something that goes beyond what Bion himself ever knew, or said, about the relevance of his own thinking to literature and aesthetics.

For Coetzee, Köhler's experiments not only lay bare a theory of thinking and a theory of literature but also give us a means of evaluating the experience of thinking and the experience of reading. Coetzee supplies an ethics by which to regard the humanity or inhumanity, the success or failure, of the problems of thinking and art. He affords us criteria for estimating literary achievement. Here is a fuller account of Costello's description of Sultan's response to Köhler's experiment, wherein Costello gives an ethical reading of Köhler's experiments through a depiction of Sultan's mind:

> Sultan knows: Now one is supposed to think. That is what the bananas up there are about. The bananas are there to make one think, to spur one to the limits of one's thinking. But what must one think? One thinks: Why is he starving me? One thinks: What have I done? Why has he stopped liking me? One thinks: Why does he not want these crates any more? But none of these is the right thought. Even a more complicated thought – for instance: What is wrong with him, what misconceptions does he have of me, that leads him to believe it is easier for me to reach a banana hanging from a wire than to pick up a banana from the floor?—is wrong. The right thought to think is: How does one use the crates to reach the bananas?

p. 72

Coetzee introduces here an ethics of thinking, and of literature, which he summarizes shortly thereafter in poignant terms:

> At every turn Sultan is driven to think the less interesting thought. From the purity of speculation (Why do men behave like this?) he is relentlessly propelled towards lower, practical, instrumental reason (How does one use this to get that?) and thus towards acceptance of himself as primarily an organism with an appetite that needs to be satisfied.
>
> *p. 73*

What is Coetzee's assessment of Köhler ethically, even aesthetically? In devising tests for the apes, Köhler has played his part in so far as he presented the conditions for thinking. This is equivalent to saying that he has presented a problem that can evoke thought. Furthermore, he has played the game fairly in so far *as he has only posed problems that indeed have solutions.* He has not tricked the apes. He has not set them impossible or unfair tasks. To do that would have been to torture them, to make them feel, as Bion describes in *Learning From Experience*, like the patient who "feels that he has feelings, but cannot learn from them; sensations ... but cannot learn from them either. A determination not to experience anything can be shown to co-exist with an inability to reject or ignore any stimulus" (p. 18). Put in such a position, Sultan could not reject any stimulus for interpretation, *and so would be left in a state of intolerable effort to solve a problem that is unsolvable.* These are the rules of war, whether you are a research psychologist, a psychoanalyst, or a fiction writer: pose fair, tolerable problems; provide the implements necessary for something that the subject would recognize as a solution, as success, as a bridge.

However, Köhler, Coetzee tells us, lost his way ethically the moment he forced Sultan to at every turn "think the less interesting thought." As Costello puts it, "In his deepest being Sultan is not interested in the banana-problem. Only the experimenter's single-minded regimentation forces him to concentrate on it" (p. 75). This is not simply a limitation placed on Sultan that keeps him trapped in his apedom; it is a form of sadism in that it trains Sultan to hate thinking. Thinking is a burden that he can only experience as bizarre and labyrinthine, much like the beta-elements that Bion tells us beset the psychotic mind. The lesson taught to Sultan is the same lesson learned by the simpleton or Fool in so many works of literature: thinking will get you nowhere in life because you are no good at it; if you can give it up completely, you should. Now that you can think, all you can think is: I am a fool. This lesson is not born of love or knowledge, but of hate and scientific devotion. Against this cruel lesson, literature usually grants the Fool some justice: he is in the end revealed as a font of wisdom, and the world to have been the Fool all along.[2]

On these grounds, Costello concludes, "Wolfgang Köhler was probably a good man. A good man but not a poet" (p. 74). He lacked, she says, "a feel for the ape's experience" (p. 74). I take this to mean that Köhler failed to grasp the aesthetic dimension of his science. As a psychologist, he worked justly, breeding the miracle of thought in a way that science would consider humane. Aesthetically, however, he failed. Köhler was not able to recognize that, just as Sultan had been tasked with crossing from apedom into humanity, he himself had been tasked with crossing over from the scientific to the poetic, from the practical to the lyric. While Sultan was stacking his boxes, Köhler was traversing the bridge which, Coetzee tells us, is "the problem of the opening," not just the opening of the novel, but an opening through which one can find one's way out of practical reason and into higher forms of thought. Sultan and his brethren managed, in the end, to think, learned to pile boxes up to reach the bananas. Köhler, for his part, was unable to think, for he did not recognize the problem that his own experiments posed to him, as a psychologist and scientist. He had no feel for Sultan's experience, and so could not traverse the bridge connecting psychology and poetry.

Coetzee's reading of Köhler, alongside the theory of literature proposed in the opening of *Elizabeth Costello*, can be read both as a cautionary tale of the fate of the psychologist who ventures haphazardly into the poetic realm (and fails to realize it, and consequently fails), and as a guideline for evaluating a work of literature that poses its aesthetics in the terms of thinking itself. I summarize these guidelines as follows. Literature very often invites thinking by presenting the reader with conditions in which thinking is called for. This is not incidental, but is central to the aesthetic function of literature. The aesthetics of literature work by making a particular kind of appeal to the intellect. This appeal to the intellect is made in the form of a problem (just as epistemological appeals are made by Köhler and Bion in the form of problems). However, there are ethically inflected rules of engagement that govern these problems. First, a problem must have a solution—in other words, the subject (the reader, in our case) must be capable of interpreting the problem in a way that alleviates the frustration of the problem. (Torture should never masquerade as a problem). Second, a problem must lead toward the more interesting thought, never the less interesting thought. We should never be led to hate thinking, or to concentrate on a problem that cannot interest us. The purpose of the problem should not be to make the reader feel a fool. Third, literature must make it possible, as Costello says, "to think ourselves into the being of another" (p. 80). We must be able to press ourselves sympathetically into the mind of the one who is attempting to solve the problem being posed, and so be capable of facing everything that the ape, the reader, the patient, faces. For we are responsible for what they face; we have designed the dusty yard of bananas and boxes, the novel, the consulting room. They are on this island because of us.

Late in his career, Bion attempted to write memoir and fiction. His most ambitious project in these areas is the philosophical novel *A Memoir of the Future*, a very long book the primary goal of which seems to be to cross the bridge from psychological epistemology to aesthetics. More specifically, the book is an attempt on Bion's part to discover what, if anything, happens to theories of thinking and dreamwork when they are contained in literary aesthetics. What happens to the problem of thinking when it is transformed into a problem of literature? In this respect, Bion is on the same journey as Köhler, though Bion was more adventurous than Köhler. Bion was willing to see to the end, in his own way, the aesthetic dimension of his scientific work, to investigate the aesthetic function that inheres in the thinking function.

There are different methods of evaluating literature, but it seems to me that the only fair method of evaluation is one that judges the work according to the terms it sets for itself. This method has the advantage of refraining from imposing a standard that is external to, or irrelevant to, the work, and also the advantage of allowing us to judge the work on the basis of how well it executes according to its own goals and procedures. It is extremely difficult to know how best to read a work like *A Memoir of the Future*, but I believe I have demonstrated that Bion's fiction must be evaluated according to the guidelines described above. This makes sense, as the guidelines above are suited for works that span science and art and are explicitly couched in epistemological terms. So, in what follows, I will apply each of the tenets presented in the guidelines above to Bion's *A Memoir of the Future* as a way of considering the relative success or failure of Bion's attempt to recast the coming into being of thinking in literary terms.

First rule: Problems posed must have solutions

It is easy to be misled by the first rule. The first rule is not supporting the notion that literature has a solution. Art has no solution; it is always in the act of expressing that aspect of itself that is irreducible, and of opposing any tendency of criticism to reduce it to formulation. However, literature must also grant the reader some way of interpreting it such that the reader is able to feel that they are in the process of solving the problem of the work. The act of solving the problem must give the reader the satisfaction of progress, must make the reader feel that his reading is truth-directed (Coetzee, 1992, p. 261). The reader must be able to learn from the experience of reading, even without any hope of coming to the end of that learning experience.

The flaw of *A Memoir of the Future* is that it poses a problem to which there is no solution. At every turn it presents the reader with a bridging problem: it presents characters that amount to beta elements exerting a pressure to which the reader wishes to develop the apparatus for reading. In the introduction, Bion asserts that in what he writes, significant meanings and rhythms are "communicated and interpretable" (p. ix); that there is a set of "rules" to which the language of the work "conforms"; and though difficult to follow they can indeed be followed. However, it seems to me that Bion here does not understand the transformation that occurs when the problem of thinking becomes the problem of literature. Bion seems to believe that, in psychological epistemology, an ability to tolerate frustration leads to the development of an apparatus for thinking, and that, transferred into the aesthetic realm, the same will occur. However, reading requires a sense of being in the process of solving the problem posed by the work. Reading is not a coping mechanism, but rather a motivated sense of building an interpretive bridge that functions as a solution. The reading apparatus does not develop in precisely the same way as the thinking apparatus. The reading apparatus solves the problem of reading: it transforms reading from a desperate response to the frustration of confusion into an active knocking together of a bridge into the aesthetic territory.

A Memoir of the Future is thinkable, but it is not readable. It offers no aesthetic solution to the problem it poses. It trades in frustration, with the expectation that frustration will inevitably breed thought. As the character Man says to the character Bion, "I am not going to do your thinking for you" (p. 161). In other words, the book will offer no relief from frustration—solve the problem of the book yourself, or starve. But the frustration, in the absence of a solution, becomes a form of torture in which the reader, as a substitute for Sultan, is led into situations in which the experiment is designed to give the sense that there is a solution to the problem when in fact there is no solution. This would be as cruel as leaving Sultan starving in a cage, bananas hung from the wire ceiling, but with boxes that he could never stack or arrange to reach his prize.

Second rule: A problem must lead toward the more interesting thought, never the less interesting thought

One of the respites of the death-by-a-thousand-cuts that is *A Memoir of the Future* is the fact that it leads the reader toward the more interesting, not the less interesting, thought. The book is in many ways a machine devised to draw one out of practical or instrumental reason and push one toward creative and metaphysical thinking. Despite all the frustration that the book foists on the reader, it does not engender in the reader a hatred, or distrust, of thinking, precisely because, where it does permit lucid thought, it does so in a way that leads the reader away from apedom and toward higher intellect. We see how this happens in the following selection:

MYSELF: What is the difference that you seem to make between 'theorising' and what you call 'practising' psycho-analysis? It seems to me that practising psycho-analysis consists of theorizing.

BION: 'Theorising' is, I admit, a part of practising psycho-analysis.

MYSELF: I think what you have just said sounds as if it makes something clear, but almost at once the illumination either turns out to be illusory and your explanation meaningless, or perhaps you have clarified a problem and the 'clarification' is at once replaced by a further series of 'unknowns.'

BION: Both are possible. That is a difficulty about 'learning'. The moment of illumination is also the moment at which it becomes clear that there is a doubt about the 'clarification' itself and about the 'matter' which it is hoped to comprehend. I think this must be a familiar experience to Sherlock Holmes.

SHERLOCK: I am not a philosopher and I don't think I can even guess what a psycho-analyst is, but since you appeal to me as if I were experienced I take it you are referring to something of which I have experience. I remember an occasion when I saw a client and I detected a strong smell of cigar about his clothes. It proved to be a valuable clue and later I wrote a monograph on ash which also turned out to be valuable, though in a way that I never expected.

p. 201

The passage reflects the deep structure of the novel: a concept (theorizing) is raised, after which it undergoes a process of interrogation that simultaneously clarifies and mystifies the concept. When one concept is tentatively proposed as equivalent to another (here theorizing is proposed as analogous to psychoanalysis), it is immediately subjected to processes meant to cast doubt on the comparison: theorizing is presented as just one "part of" psychoanalysis, but this refinement (rather than leading down a path toward further clarity) is immediately accused of being a charade (clarification is undone by a "series of unknowns"). Every clarification is negated by the fact that the clarification only serves to introduce unknowns. This dialectic of elucidation and mystification functions as a motor by which the less interesting thought (what one believes is true) is transformed into a more interesting thought (what one believed was true is now revealed to be only partially true), and then into an even more interesting thought (that elucidation and stupefaction are in fact two side of the same coin, each bringing the other into being). The entire book is a kind of machine for spurring the thinking apparatus to greater and greater heights. The thinking function proliferates even as the aesthetic function falters.

Third rule: He who designs the problem of the book must be able to think his way "into the being of another"

Coetzee calls the capacity to think one's way into another's being the "sympathetic imagination" (2004, p. 80). This is not simply the ability to picture oneself behaving like Sultan, but the ability to inhabit Sultan such that one would know what it was like for Sultan to be Sultan. Though a human can never be an ape, he can inhabit the mind of an ape if he can spur himself to exercise the sympathetic imagination. Much as Sultan is drawn into human thinking (made to think as if he were a human, not just behave as if he were thinking like a human), so must the author be able to follow Sultan backwards, so to speak, as he leaves the human territory and returns into his ape being.

A Memoir of the Future is an interesting test case with regard to the third rule. The book opens with a dialogue that speaks to the relationship between author and reader:

Q: Can you give me an idea what this is about?
A: Psycho-analysis, I believe.
Q: Are you sure? It looks a queer affair.
A: It is a queer affair—like psycho-analysis. You'd have to read it.
Q: How much does it cost?
A: It says it on the book. You would have to read it as well though.
Q: Of course. But I don't think I can afford the time or money.
A: Nor do I.
Q: But haven't you read it?
A: Yes, in a way.
Q: You're a queer salesman. I'm only wanting to know …

A: I'm not the salesman. I only wrote it.
Q: Oh, I beg your pardon! I quite thought …
A: I'm flattered, but I'm only the author.
Q: May I have your autograph?
A: No.
Q: Oh.

p. 2

Bion is right to insist here that a writer is a reader but in a way that is different from how a reader who is not a writer is a reader. A writer reads what he writes "in a way": He reads as writer. Bion is establishing from the outset that a reader ("Q")—particularly one who is so naïve as to think that a work is about some idea—will never be a reader in the way that the author ("A") is a reader. Q is, really, every reader who is not A, and Q is decisively excluded from the possibility of reading.

Another way of putting this is that Bion is both A and Q. Bion is not trying to think his way into another's being, but into his own being. His sympathetic imagination does not extend outward, but inward. We, as readers (as "Q"s) are on the outside looking in—we ask the wrong questions, we want something from the book that it can't give us. We are not so much readers of Bion's book but witnesses to Bion's reading of himself—his attempt to inhabit himself *imaginatively*. *A Memoir of the Future* is not really a problem posed to the reader, but a problem posed by Bion to himself as reader. If there is a touch of genius in the book (along with many touches of failure), it is in how Bion has taken the age-old task of empathizing with another's experience and transformed it into perhaps the more novel task of inhabiting one's own mind, of imagining what it is like for I to be I. Bion speaks directly to this challenge here:

> MYSELF: Since I cannot, for all my experience, analytic or other than analytic, say who I am, I know now that it is very unlikely that I shall know any better at some future date. It is impossible to believe anyone who is not me will know better. I am sure it would be useful if I knew who that person is that I am compelled to be as long as I exist.
>
> *p. 131*

The philosophy of self here is convoluted, but amounts to the self acknowledging that it is both its own sole author and sole reader, both A and Q. The mind is a problem posed to itself, just as for Bion the literary work is a work written for the writer who reads. Though there is an auto-destructive cleverness to a work that presents itself in this way, there is also an exhaustive solipsism. After the prefatory dialogue between A and Q, the novel opens with the statement, "I am tired" (p. 3). And it seems that there is, for nearly eight hundred pages, a weariness born of the torment of being asked to read a book we are told we cannot read and solve a problem for which there is no solution. Led again and again into the yard, Sultan no doubt felt as the reader does when faced with so much self-flagellating thinking: "I am tired."

At one level, *A Memoir of the Future* falls short of its purported goal of submitting psychoanalytic epistemology to aesthetic epistemology. As I have tried to demonstrate, *Memoir* creates a reader only to punish or exclude him, which if we follow analogous theories of thinking (the cognitive behavioral theory of Köhler and the aesthetic theory of Coetzee) is a violation of the contract that holds sway over researcher and subject, or author and reader. And yet, at another level, Bion's work, as entrapped as it is in the ineluctable conventions of thinking and literary aesthetics, is also able to serve as a rebellion against preexistent rules and expectations. The Epilogue to *Memoir* addresses this aspect of the book:

> All my life I have been imprisoned, frustrated, dogged by common-sense, reason, memories, desires and—greatest bug-bear of all—understanding and being understood. This is an attempt to express my rebellion, to say 'Good-bye' to all that. It is my wish, I now realize doomed to failure, to write a book unspoiled by any tincture of common-sense, reason, etc. (see above). So although I would write, 'Abandon Hope all ye who expect to find any facts— scientific, aesthetic or religious—in this book', I cannot claim to have succeeded. All these will, I fear, be seen to have left their traces, vestiges, ghosts hidden within these words; even sanity, like 'cheerfulness', will creep in. However successful my attempt, there would always be the risk that the book 'became' acceptable, respectable, honoured and unread. 'Why write then?' you may ask. To prevent someone who KNOWS from filling the empty space—but I fear I am being 'reasonable', that great Ape. Wishing you all a Happy Lunacy and a Relativistic Fission …
>
> *p. 578*

Bion here identifies as central to *Memoir* the concerns, feelings, and problems that I found in his work via Köhler: the problem of being "imprisoned"; a sense of doom and dread borne of unceasing frustration; a streak of sadism (captured above in the allusion to Dante); an awe-inspiring pointlessness that is the heart of an 800-page book that can't be read. But Bion here announces that, though he is forever haunted by the traces of established formulae and conventions, he will do his best to live as outlaw—to live outside of all the laws, and boxes, and camps. The "great Ape" for Bion is he who is "reasonable," a being who is led to solve the problem in front of him without questioning the terms of the problem itself. He who rebels against this expectation emerges from his apedom into human life.

In several places in *The Mentality of Apes*, Köhler recounts moments when the apes grow enraged. They kick at the boxes, snarl, flagellate themselves. The descriptions are painful to read, because one understands the torment and frustration that drives the chimpanzees to wish that the world would stop demanding so much from them. Bion, in the above passage, supplies a kinder reading of these irate fits of the apes: that Sultan and his fellow apes were exhibiting their own kind of rebellion, one that expressed the wise thinking that inheres in the ability to reject knowing and live less knowingly. They were not being driven mad by a malevolent game, but erupting in brave rebellion.

Notes

1 This chapter was published in the collection *Bion in Contemporary Psychoanalysis: Reading a Memoir of the Future* (Routledge, 2017).
2 For further discussion of the Fool as literary figure, see the chapter "The Risk of True Confession," particularly the section devoted to the mystery of thinking.

PART III

Losing, thinking, dreaming

4

HOW LANGUAGE HOLDS LOSS

On literature and a lost corner of the mind

There is no more important function of the human mind than to make losses that are permanent bearable, and to make losses that may be temporary bearable until the moment of being reunited with what has been lost. One cannot really be alive if one is unable to suffer loss, as being alive entails losing aspects of that aliveness and, finally, losing all of that aliveness in death. We no doubt learn to bear permanent and impermanent losses differently, but in either case we must develop the best understanding we can of the human experience of losing—what it is like to lose, what challenges losing poses, whether finding is the end of losing, and so on.

At the core of this matter is the pain of losing itself and the difficulty of expressing this pain. Not only is it, of course, difficult to talk about what pains us, but in the case of losing we also face the challenge of communicating the depth and specificity of what has been lost—of articulating and making clear just what the lost object meant to us, and, at the same time, all that the lost object meant to us. This need to express so much exerts a pressure on the words in which loss is spoken or written. Loss, I find when I study expressions of it, stretches language to its limits, as the speaker tries to put more and more of all that has been lost into language, which for all its volume, has no unit that is infinite (a sentence is not infinite; a paragraph is not; a page not; a book not).

For this reason, I find that expressions of loss rely more heavily on voice and tone and lilt and modulation than do expressions of other large emotions. Happiness, anger, jealousy: these are told and heard, while loss is sung and listened to. Loss seems to have the same relationship to language and mind as air does to a wind instrument: it passes through the firm structures of language and mind, and this passing through becomes the sound of the instrument. There is, then, a kind of instrument in the mind, made of mental structures and the grammar of language, through which experience of loss passes, with the sound of each loss determined by the particular instrument (the specific psyche and language of the individual) and the unique application of air (the form that the will to express loss takes at any given moment). The one who loses asks himself: "Can he love her enough to write a music for her?" (Coetzee 1999, p. 182). And so when one attends a wake or a funeral, one hears the oddest, most complex cacophony of wails, whimpers, moans, whispers, chuckles, shifts, and sniffles. The sound of a funeral or wake says more about what the dead meant to the audience than do the works spoken in commemoration of the dead.

Just listen to the opening three stanzas of Elizabeth Bishop's poem "One Art" (1983):

> The art of losing isn't hard to master;
> so many things seem filled with the intent
> to be lost that their loss is no disaster.
>
> Lose something every day. Accept the fluster
> of lost door keys, the hour badly spent.
> The art of losing isn't hard to master.
>
> Then practice losing farther, losing faster:
> places, and names, and where it was you meant
> to travel. None of these will bring disaster.
>
>   *p. 178, l. 1–9*

This poem is indeed a technical accomplishment (it carries off a variation of the difficult villanelle), as well as an aching meditation on the nature of loss. But it is the tone of the refrain that makes the poem: "The art of losing isn't hard to master." If you try to say that phrase out loud in the same way multiple times, you will find that it is impossible to repeat the phrase in exactly the same way as you did the time before. Each reading is a little different. The emotion of the sentence— acting, when spoken, like the air that passes through an instrument—touches the sentence a bit differently upon each reading. Sometimes, when I read it, the sentence is grave; sometimes it is ironic; sometimes it is almost smug, particularly when I read it as an ever-so-arrogant boast. Sometimes the stress falls more heavily on "art" than on any other word, while at other times nearly every other word could be given the stress: "losing," "isn't," "hard," "master." When the sentence is read as part of the entire poem, the word "master" catches, depending on the reading, the flapping of one of the words with which it is rhymed ("disaster," "fluster," "faster"). "One Art" is not so much a poem about losing as a poem that is written in the voice of losing; every word lives out the impossible, very sad art form that is mastered by those fortunate enough to live through each successive stage in the natural life cycle.

But it is also important that the voice of losing not fall back on tired, unoriginal platitudes. The "art of losing" that Bishop sings of is her own creation—it comes from an instrument unique to her experiences of loss, and she creates this instrument as a poet in a way that is different from every other instrument of loss. There is a moment in J.M. Coetzee's novel *Disgrace* (1999) when the protagonist, David Lurie, is struggling to come up with the music for a chamber opera depicting the dull middle-aged life of the Contessa Teresa Guiccioli, the mistress and now widow of Lord Byron, as she laments that the sole fiery part of her life is now over. Lurie at first tries to express the loss in words:

> Working as swiftly as he can, holding tight to Teresa, he tries to sketch out the opening pages of a libretto. Get the words down on paper, he tells himself. Once that is done it will all be easier. Then there will be time to search through the masters—through Gluck, for instance—lifting melodies, perhaps—who knows?—lifting ideas too.
>
> *p. 183*

Actually it is not enough, Lurie discovers, to resurrect dead words and ideas:

> But by steps, as he begins to live his days more fully with Teresa and the dead Byron, it becomes clear that purloined songs will not be good enough, that the two will demand a music of their own. And, astonishingly, in dribs and drabs, the music comes. Sometimes the contour of a phrase occurs to him before he has a hint of what the words themselves will be; sometimes the words call forth the cadence; sometimes the shade of a melody, having hovered for days on the edge of hearing, unfolds and blessedly reveals itself. As the action begins to unwind, furthermore, it calls up of its own accord modulations and transitions that he feels in his blood even when he has not the musical resources to realize them.
>
> *p. 183*

Such is the state of one who is trying to express loss: he is trying to invent a music which can carry all of what he has emotionally in his blood; often, words will become overburdened because, lacking the musical resources to express everything, he will try to pack into language what he cannot express in sound. But what is most important is that, as is the case between analyst and patient, writer and reader, the two will "demand a music of their own." As E.M. Forster said, "One death may explain itself, but it throws no light upon another" (1921, p. 276). Each death, each loss, requires its own explanation, which will include an understanding of how a loss explains itself. And loss, as in Bishop's refrain, can often be found expressed in the most minute trembling of tones, "at the edge of hearing" where the "art of losing"—in its many varieties—is on display.

Loss, then, brings together the exigencies of precise expression of vast emotion and the resources of sound for putting into language so much emotion. This coming together brings us into the realm of poetry. The poet George Quasha speaks wisely when he says, "The role of poetry is to do what language can't, or won't, otherwise do" (2015, p. 132). Loss, we may say, is often articulated at a point where language is pushed into contortions, made to assume "stress positions" in which it must bear more than it is normally expected to bear. Loss exerts a pressure on language, denaturing it to the point where it is asked to do things that language either can't do, or would never do otherwise. Consider the opening stanza of Emily Dickinson's "A Loss of Something Ever Felt I—":

> A loss of something ever felt I—
> The first that I could recollect
> Bereft I was—of what I knew not
> Too young that any should suspect
> *2007, p. 959, l. 1–4*

Language almost cannot do what Dickinson makes it do in this first line. The language of the sentence is, typical of Dickinson, bracing, stunned, but profoundly alive, like a little bird that has flown into a window but survived. The words are arranged in a sequence that has the effect of short-circuiting grammar's function of involuntarily delivering language in such a way that it can be processed in chunks and involuntarily understood. Rather, the words seem to be put down one by one, guided by a faint syntactical coherence. "Ever" would seem, at first read, to establish a temporal structure to hang on to, but at second reading I am not sure what "ever" does to clarify, or situate, "a loss of something." But nonetheless, the "ever" gets between what has been lost ("something") and the one who felt the loss ("felt I—"), so that it serves to strain—by separating the lost object and the one who lost the object in both time and diction—the expression of personal loss. The dash at the end of the line is a silence that makes a sound, as we hear the awkwardness of ending an independent clause with "I—." Language would not, as Quasha says, "otherwise do" this.

Again, language is stretched to its breaking point—reworked from its very foundations so as not to burst into nonsense—in an effort to deal with the demands that loss places on language. Part of the "art of losing" (of making art from loss and losing artfully) is calling upon all the resources of language—including resources rarely called upon—to not only contain the complex emotions of loss, but also to bring to bear all the resources of sound and music to round out and complete expressions of loss.

In writing, and this is often true in psychoanalysis, the "art of losing"—the capacity to call up, or develop anew, language that expresses *all* that the lost object meant, and *just* what the lost object meant—is also an art of not losing. Writing, even if we use it to put certain lost things to rest, is also how we keep from having to lose entirely. And yet, we also know that as much as writing preserves, it also puts the final cup of dirt on the grave. Loss, psychologically and aesthetically, is a race between mastery ("the art of losing," with its tight poetic forms holding the shape of what is gone) and disaster (either the failure of art to preserve or memorialize, or despair at how hollow art can be as consolation for a devastating loss). Bishop shows this quite perfectly:

The art of losing isn't hard to master;
so many things seem filled with the intent
to be lost that their loss is no disaster.

"Master" and "disaster" are rhymed, both because rhyme turns them into poetic fellows thereby neutralizing disaster through art, and because mastery, in a world in which all life is "filled with the intent" to die, is a disaster. Just look at how the poem ends:

I lost my mother's watch. And look! my last, or
next-to-last, of three loved houses went.
The art of losing isn't hard to master.

I lost two cities, lovely ones. And, vaster,
some realms I owned, two rivers, a continent.
I miss them, but it wasn't a disaster.

—Even losing you (the joking voice, a gesture
I love) I shan't have lied. It's evident
the art of losing's not too hard to master
though it may look like (*Write* it!) like disaster.
            p. 178, l. 10–19

The poem widens into whimsy ("some realms I owned"), then grows brash at the prospect of giving up the whole world ("I miss them, but it wasn't a disaster.") But it is in the final stanza that we see loss place its greatest demand upon art. The final quatrain is a Frankenstein's monster of dashes, interjections, silly archaisms ("shan't"), and stuttering repetitions. The stanza begins with a Dickinsonian dash of quiet and ends with "disaster" (the limits of the loss are drawn between silent oblivion and roaring grief). Forced between spluttering stammering ("like...like") we get an injunction ("*Write* it!") that is more a gasping for air than a drawing of breath. The critic J.D. McClatchy (1989) is right when he says:

The whole stanza is in danger of breaking apart, and breaking down. In this last line the poet's voice literally cracks. The villanelle—that strictest and most intractable of verse forms—can barely control the grief, yet helps the poet keep her balance.
            p. 145

Whereas the fourth and fifth stanzas begin with statements that say what happened without showing us anything of feeling ("I lost" repeats), the final stanza pictures for us the insides of losing, where any and every attempt to hold together is eaten through by the corrosive that is the unstaunchable flow of loss.

Had I not recently visited Mexico City, and the Blue House where Frida Kahlo and Diego Rivera lived, I would have thought that nothing could be done about language's relationship to loss; that language has no alternative but to brace itself when faced with the task of expressing deep loss, and that art could only be a momentary stay against an ineluctable force. But consider: "Perhaps they expect me to wail and moan about 'how much I suffer,' living with Diego. But I don't think that the banks of a river suffer by letting it flow … ."[1] This is Kahlo speaking about Diego Rivera, her frequently awful husband. At first, we think that what Kahlo objects to is the expectation that her pain and loss will be expressed in moans and wails. But this is not what she objects to. What she objects to is the notion that art and language suffer for having to express suffering. Far from being the case, according to Kahlo, language will no more suffer for having pain run through it than a river will suffer for letting water run through it. This is not a statement about rivers, of course, but a statement about herself. Kahlo's life was pain upon pain; her childhood polio and the terrible injury she suffered in a bus accident when she was 18 years old left her in unending agony, subject to one surgery after another. In her private studio she hung upon the wall a large poster of the pre-natal stages of the intrauterine growth of a baby, as if to display before her every step of what she had lost when her accident rendered her unable to bear children. Her husband cheated on her repeatedly, most cruelly with her sister.

Art, for Kahlo, did not suffer for having to contain so much loss and grief. That is what it is there for. Art is not a mastery of loss, or even a diversion, but the shape that loss takes when we try to express it, or release it, or hold on to it. This shape is not something imposed upon life by art. Due to her debilitating injury, Kahlo had to wear a series of corsets in the second half of her life because her spine was too weak to support her body. These corsets—which, with their straps and rigid plaster, seem like punitive apparatuses more than support structures—are displayed behind glass at the Blue House. What Kahlo did with these corsets is paint upon them the most marvelous designs, every bit as beautiful and aesthetically complex as those we see in her paintings. I do not think it is correct to say that she was turning loss into art with her designs. That would be to make art into a mastery of loss, which would be to violate Kahlo's belief that art is not a mastery of loss but the banks through which its stream winds. The corset, left blank, is already the shape that loss takes, and the painful contortion into which the corset forces the human body is already a binding of human loss. It is not art that suffers, but the human shaped inside of art.

Expressions of loss, from this perspective, are not so much corsets made of language to contain loss. Rather, expressions of loss are designs written upon the corsets. These designs can, in the end, do nothing to master loss; they are not meant to master it. We think we are building the corset, when the corset in fact holds the loss together already, allowing us a shape on which to impress images of what is being held inside. Language, rather paradoxically, is something we write on, not in. Loss already takes the shape of language. With this shape, we can do what we wish, wailing in agony if that is what is occurring inside the corset, or bracing for worse to come, if that is what is happening, or imagining the corset rupturing, if that is what we worry will happen, as in the case of the greatest physical and emotional distresses. When the corset breaks completely, then we are dead, and the art is preserved in shreds until such a time as it disintegrates, or no one is left who is interested in being a caretaker of shreds.

★★★

So far, I have tried to show how in literature, and I think in psychoanalysis too, some of the psychology and experience of loss is expressed. An understanding of the expression of loss is also helpful in learning to listen to loss, and for loss, and to developing an "art of losing" in which one can express the extent of loss without fearing that the breakdown of language is a breakdown in the ability to grieve.

But, as I said, we have looked at only snippets, and more can be learned from a full scene of losing, including how the mind makes sense of what is lost and how it picks up again with a lost object once that object has been found. Much of what I believe to be true about the psychological operations of loss I grew convinced of reading the novel *Never Let Me Go* (2005), by the Japanese-born British writer, Kazuo Ishiguro, and so I will turn to a scene from this novel for a lengthier depiction of the psychology of loss. Whether indeed the mind works in the way Ishiguro has it work in this part of his novel is, I believe, irrelevant to one's ability to learn from what he has written, for he has at the very least found the language to express a mind, and ultimately what we are interested in is how to understand any mind that crosses our path, whether we have seen one like it before or not, whether we will ever see another like it again.

That Kazuo Ishiguro would be fascinated with loss and its recreation into music is no surprise given his childhood and the unusual kind of loss he suffered during it. Ishiguro was born in Japan in 1954, and lived there until he was five years old, at which point he moved with his parents to England. His father was an oceanographer, with a two-year research opportunity at the National Institute of Oceanography in Guildford, a small town in Southern England. Though he was just five years old when he left Japan, it was a painful emigration because he was forced to leave his grandfather, with whom he was very close. Despite the difficulty of their relocation, there was every expectation that the family would only be in England for a few years, so Ishiguro was raised with Japanese values and traditions, speaking only Japanese at home. The implication was that they were visiting England, not living there forever. However, their return to Japan kept on getting postponed, as Ishiguro's father's position was extended again and again. Despite the fact that the family's stay in England took on a feeling of permanence with each renewal of his father's contract, throughout his childhood there was an expectation that at some point Ishiguro and his parents would return to Japan. After some years, however, the truth grew too obvious to ignore: they would never return to Japan. Ishiguro, for reasons that still seem obscure to me, chose not to return to Japan, even to visit, for thirty years. Even so, his first two novels, *A Pale View of Hills* (1982) and *An Artist of the Floating World* (1986), are set in Japan, and written years before he was to visit Japan as an adult. He wrote about what he lost instead of returning for what he lost; or he returned in art rather than by plane. It is enough to say that Ishiguro's mind was formed by losses that were partial, delayed, hidden, irremediable, and generally confusing.[2]

To understand how Ishiguro describes loss, one must know the premise of *Never Let Me Go*: Kathy H., the narrator, is a clone, as are her friends Tommy and Ruth, and all the other children with whom she grows up. They don't have mothers and fathers. They have only "possibles": the men or women from whom they are genetically derived. Though Ishiguro never tells us exactly how many clones there are in this futuristic Britain, we get the impression that there are thousands of them, raised in special schools all throughout England. Tommy, Ruth, and Kathy are friends, and occasional lovers, at shining Hailsham, the best of all the schools, the one that all clones speak of with the reverence associated with a Harvard or an Oxford. Britain created these clones, we learn, so that their organs can be harvested and used by the public. The lives of these clones are decided for them: once they have finished their schooling (which stops at high school age), most of them will become "donors," giving away organ after organ to the general population until they "complete" (a euphemism for dying). About this fate of theirs they are, as one of their Hailsham instructors puts it, "told and not told" (p. 81): they are both informed of their purpose and kept from knowing its full, awful, unjust meaning. A few of them can defer donations for a time by becoming a "carer," which involves assisting other clones in their donations, which become increasingly painful and risky as each subsequent organ is bequeathed to Britain. Carers eventually become donors. Kathy is an experienced carer, and narrates the novel from the perspective of one in that particular position.

In the scene below, Kathy tells of the fate of a precious cassette tape that she lost when she was a girl, and of the circumstances under which she "found" it again many years later in a town called Norfolk:

> I still have a copy of that tape and until recently I'd listen to it occasionally driving out in the open country on a drizzly day. But now the tape machine in my car's got so dodgy, I don't dare play it in that. And there never seems enough time to play it when I'm back in my bedsit. Even so, it's one of my precious possessions. Maybe come the end of the year, when I'm no longer a carer, I'll be able to listen to it more often.
>
> The album's called *Songs After Dark* and it's by Judy Bridgewater. What I've got today isn't the actual cassette, the one I had back then at Hailsham, the one I lost. It's the one Tommy and I found in Norfolk years afterwards—but that's another story I'll come to later. What I want to talk about is the first tape, the one that disappeared.
>
> I should explain before I go any further this whole thing we had in those days about Norfolk. We kept it going for years and years—it became a sort of in-joke, I suppose—and it all started from one particular lesson we had when we were pretty young.
>
> It was Miss Emily herself who taught us about the different counties of England. She'd pin up a big map over the blackboard, and next to it, set up an

easel. And if she was talking about, say, Oxfordshire, she'd place on the easel a large calendar with photos of the county. She had quite a collection of these picture calendars, and we got through most of the counties this way. She'd tap a spot on the map with her pointer, turn to the easel and reveal another picture. There'd be little villages with streams going through them, white monuments on hillsides, old churches beside fields; if she was telling us about a coastal place, there'd be beaches crowded with people, cliffs with seagulls. I suppose she wanted us to have a grasp of what was out there surrounding us, and it's amazing, even now, after all these miles I've covered as a carer, the extent to which my idea of the various counties is still set by these pictures Miss Emily put up on her easel. I'd be driving through Derbyshire, say, and catch myself looking for a particular village green with a mock-Tudor pub and a war memorial—and realise it's the image Miss Emily showed us the first time I ever heard of Derbyshire.

Anyway, the point is, there was a gap in Miss Emily's calendar collection: none of them had a single picture of Norfolk. We had these same lectures repeated a number of times, and I'd always wonder if this time she'd found a picture of Norfolk, but it was always the same. She'd wave her pointer over the map and say, as a sort of afterthought: "And over here, we've got Norfolk. Very nice there."

Then, that particular time, I remember how she paused and drifted off into thought, maybe because she hadn't planned what should happen next instead of a picture. Eventually she came out of her dream and tapped the map again.

"You see, because it's stuck out here on the east, on this hump jutting into the sea, it's not on the way to anywhere. People going north and south"—she moved the pointer up and down—"they bypass it altogether. For that reason, it's a peaceful corner of England, rather nice. But it's also something of a lost corner."

A lost corner. That's what she called it, and that was what started it. Because at Hailsham, we had our own "Lost Corner" up on the third floor, where the lost property was kept; if you lost or found anything, that's where you went. Someone—I can't remember who it was—claimed after the lesson that what Miss Emily had said was that Norfolk was England's "lost corner," where all the lost property found in the country ended up. Somehow this idea caught on and soon had become accepted fact virtually throughout our entire year.

p. 64

Kathy lost a cassette that was very precious to her when she was a girl. This cassette—*Songs After Dark* by Judy Bridgewater—was itself a copy, one of thousands of copies physically identical to it, containing the same cover art, exactly the same music. Like her, it is a clone. Kathy, at this moment, is describing the feelings she has about what she lost. Her profession as a carer for clones (human copies) extends to the care she takes to find the best words in which to communicate her experience with having failed to care for another kind of copy—a cassette tape—that was precious to her and which she lost. We are again seeing a person finding a language for loss. Though in this case, language is not decimated by loss, but has been enlarged by Kathy's professional humanity so as to be able to adapt to the specific dimensions of the loss in need of words.

Everything eventually is lost, so the attitude by which we deal with a lost object is the attitude in which we can face life itself. Ishiguro does not hide this fact: Kathy's relationship to a lost copy of *Songs After Dark* is nothing less than her relationship to all the copies amongst whom she lives, and to herself as a copy. And yet, the experience she has of this clone is particular—to her it is an original, and the fact that there are thousands of identical copies does nothing to lessen her love of it.

So when the cassette disappears, Kathy has lost something that exists in thousands of identical forms all over England. And yet, not having marked the cassette in any way, she has no way of knowing that any single copy of *Songs After Dark* is her copy, the original. This is a problem. The lost object (the original) is gone forever—not destroyed, but disappeared as a thing that one could recognize as original. It has gone back into circulation. One wants to see the original, but one has no way of telling it from a copy. It would be natural to despair in such a situation. Kathy not only lost an object that to her was special; she allowed a copy that she had made original to her though love to become a copy again. And for many years, some of which are described in the novel, the loss of the tape is a torment to her.

However, for reasons that are at the core of the scene, Kathy is not undone by her loss. Instead, she develops an art of losing of her own. Despite acknowledging that the "actual" tape she lost is gone forever, Kathy is able to say that, when with Tommy in Norfolk, they "found" that tape again. We must wonder how this can be. From one perspective, she did not find her lost tape. She merely found another copy of it, one of thousands exactly like it, utterly ordinary. But, for a reason that must be investigated, she makes out that she "found" the lost tape. The reason that this is so is because the lost cassette cannot be understood apart from the thing that plays the tape. Look at the opening again: "I still have a copy of that tape and until recently I'd listen to it occasionally driving out in the open country on a drizzly day. But now the tape machine in my car's got so dodgy, I don't dare play it in that." Kathy has the copy, but she cannot play it because she does not "trust" the tape player to play it safely and properly. But this is just a physical matter representing an emotional matter. Emotionally, the significance of the tape also requires playing. For this clone-tape to bear its originality it must be played *by her*. As an object, the tape is unplayable, merely a copy; as an object for her, it is playable, its full significance something that could be played. The original, in this respect, is not lost. And so the language in which Kathy describes the circumstances around the loss of this tape, and what the tape meant to her, becomes the means by which she plays the music inside the lost object. Kathy's language, both in this passage and in later scenes in which her feelings surrounding the tape are explored further, sings all that is on that tape—its profound meaning to her childhood, her sense of losing out on the chance to ever be a mother—and just what is on that tape—the songs that she, alone, listened to in her room as a girl. Most importantly, she can play the song "Never Let Me Go," which she imagined to be a song in which a woman who was told she could never have children by some miracle has a baby, and with a mixture of profound love and fear of losing the child, sings to it, again and again, "Baby, *baby*, never let me go…" (p. 71).

It makes sense now that Kathy's language would not burst at the seams in the process of containing such loss, for Kathy must be able to hold the tape safely before she can begin to release its music. If she does not trust herself as a tape player for the original object, she will not be able to experience the tape as any-thing more than a version of what she lost. If, however, she can trust herself as a tape player, then she will feel safe playing the specific music of this specific object. This music, however, is not literally the music of the tape, but the expression of the meaning of the tape, the meaning of the song, its place in her life. The song means what it means to her, even if that meaning has little to do with what the song was actually about. As Kathy said about what the tape meant to her, as a clone unable to ever bear children, when she listened to it:

> Even at the time, I realized this couldn't be right, that this interpretation didn't fit with the rest of the lyrics. But that wasn't an issue with me. The song was about what I said, and I used to listen to it again and again, on my own, whenever I got the chance.
>
> *p. 71*

To find something is not, then, to be reunited with it. To find something is to hear the music again of what was lost, and to hear it because you have become a mind in which that lost object can be "played." In such cases, one becomes a carer of what was lost, bringing to life for a spell something whose life would otherwise mutely spill away. Kathy "finds" her tape again only in the sense that she discovers that she is able to call up the music inside the physical object. Her capacity to bring out the tape's music is one way she is a carer in relation to herself, and is an extension of her ability to make every clone under her care sing even though she cannot keep them alive for ever. Yes, it is true that she only can call up this music once she comes upon another copy of *Songs After Dark*, but this is so as to illustrate something about physical copies, not, certainly, to illustrate that we can only play lost objects if we find facsimiles of them in the real world. We may be able to play a lost object even if we never find a thing like it ever again.

Still, we do have to do something psychologically to be able to play lost objects. It is, Ishiguro goes on to suggest, a thing the mind does. Miss Emily teaches Kathy and the other children the counties of England by showing them a picture of each county. The pictures come from a calendar, which fixes time by giving it linear order. The calendar is leant against an easel, an instrument of art. Verisimilitude is propped up by artistic imagination, just as Kathy's sense of where she is in England is propped up by her earliest memory of seeing a single representation of that part of England. She cannot see the landscape for the memory. The reproduction outstrips the original.

Nonetheless, for Kathy, this quixotic overlapping of memory and reality is little more than an amusement. She feels its relevance to herself, but one can't venture down every winding road. That's for readers to do, not characters. Kathy's true interest is in Norfolk—it's why she remembers Miss Emily's lesson at all.[3] But Norfolk, we learn, isn't actually a place. In Kathy's narrow world, a place is a picture, one example of a thousand identical tableaux available in quaintly drab British calendar art. A place is no different from some copy of *Songs After Dark* that lacked the significance that could allow her to find it and play its music.

Norfolk is, rather, an aspect of the human mind. We should not dwell on the obvious (that, crudely, Norfolk could be turned into a pale and provisional version of the unconscious) for that will only illustrate what we already know about the mind, rather than following Ishiguro to what only he knew, as a writer, when he wrote this scene. What seems most important is that this part of the mind is always awaiting loss, preparing for it, girding itself for what will eventually happen. It exists specifically to prepare us. In this way, it works against language, or, depending on how you look at it, in league with language. Language, as presented by Bishop and Dickinson though less so than by Kahlo, is stressed to the breaking point by loss and so seems forever unprepared for it. Loss is a kind of test, or torture, of language—it disfigures it. This aspect of the mind, conversely, is prepared to lose. It is not surprised by loss. Ishiguro captures both the absurdity and the utter necessity of such a part of the mind when, a few paragraphs later, Kathy says of their theory about Norfolk:

> This might all sound daft, but you have to remember that to us, at that stage in our lives, any place beyond Hailsham was like a fantasy land; we had only the haziest notions of the world outside and about what was and wasn't possible there. Besides, we never bothered to examine our Norfolk theory in any detail. What was important to us, as Ruth said one evening when we were sitting in that tiled room in Dover, looking out at the sunset, was that "when we lost something precious, and we'd looked and looked and still couldn't find it, then we didn't have to be completely heartbroken. We still had that last bit of comfort, thinking that one day, when we were grown up, and we were free to travel around the country, we could always go and find it again in Norfolk."
>
> *p. 66*

It is not difficult to see some of the tools humans have to develop and safeguard the part of the mind represented here by Norfolk (fantasy, mythopoesis, friendship). However, the mysterious nature of this part of the mind is what really forms the centerpiece of the scene. What allows the mind, as captured in the symbol of Norfolk, to be so prepared for loss?

Here, again, is the moment Miss Emily gives her lesson on Norfolk:

> "You see, because it's stuck out here on the east, on this hump jutting into the sea, it's not on the way to anywhere. People going north and south"—she

moved the pointer up and down—"they bypass it altogether. For that reason, it's a peaceful corner of England, rather nice. But it's also something of a lost corner."

p. 65

The important thing about Norfolk is that "it's not on the way to anywhere." Whereas the rest of the scene gradually reveals information so as to give the reader a feeling of understanding about Norfolk and its origins, this remarkable phrase humbles all that knowing at the feet of a beautiful mystery. "It's not on the way to anywhere." There is no end to what this sentence could mean, and yet its indeterminateness does not sway the reader from feeling it is determinately true.

But I believe, at times, that I can say what Ishiguro means; of course he hasn't given us an aporia. What he means is that when you are going to Norfolk, you are going *there*, not anyplace else. You are not going in a direction—north or south, east or west—but you are going to Norfolk, and that may be a place inside oneself. And because Norfolk is special in this very specific way, it's also a "peaceful corner." If it were on the way to somewhere, it would grow busy, and in no time would cease to be a lost corner. Norfolk, to serve its function, must be a place not on the way to anywhere else, must be peaceful and free of busyness, and must be a place in which lost objects are found beyond any reasonable expectation and played once again. This aspect of the mind recalls the analytic space, as it does literature itself.

Kathy's language, which is both formed by her experience as a carer and the reason she makes such a good carer in the first place, has a conscientious wisdom to it that allows it to softly restrain the loss that tries to overrun it. Loss can't denature such language. Norfolk seems to stand behind such language, helping language to brace for loss by growing more measured (less busy), and so more peaceful and capacious. But in doing so, something is lost. Frida Kahlo, like Kathy, dreamed of having children but could not because of a physical calamity for which she was not responsible. Kathy, following her natural gifts, learned to find the music that she lost by developing the Norfolk of her mind and by finding a language in which to express loss. Kahlo had no Norfolk. There was no place she could imagine going to recover what she lost. And so her language hardened into a corset. This, I imagine, was to the detriment of her happiness. But it was not to the detriment of her art. Her corsets made a tight boundary out of turbulent pain, and the designs she made on those corsets reflected the wailing and agony inside of her. Had she had a Norfolk in her mind, had she had a language not so tightly strapped, she could not have stood or moved, for the corset held her spine straight as much as it held together her loss.

Notes

1 This quote is stenciled onto the wall of a room in the Blue House.

2 The details of this biography have been gathered from a number of sources, namely the collection of interviews, *Conversations with Kazuo Ishiguro* (2008).
3 See the previous chapter's discussion of literature and mystery. Norfolk, within the economy of this part of the novel, is that which cannot be converted into a known quantity. If it were to become a place like all the others—a page on a calendar—it would lose its mystery and its value to Ishiguro would be exhausted.

5

THINKING IN TARJEI VESAAS' *THE BIRDS*

Below is the opening scene of Tarjei Vesaas' novel *The Birds* ([1957]2016):

Mattis looked to see if the sky was clear and free of clouds this evening, and it was. Then he said to his sister Hege, to cheer her up: "You're like lightning."

The word sent a cold shiver down his spine, but he felt safe all the same, seeing the sky was perfect.

"With those knitting needles of yours, I mean," he added. Hege nodded unconcerned and went on with the large sweater she was making. Her knitting needles were flashing. She was working on an enormous eight-petaled rose which would soon sit between the shoulders of some man.

"Yes, I know," she said simply. "But then I'm really grateful for all you do, Hege."

He was slowly tapping his knee with his middle finger—the way he always did when he was thinking. Up and down, up and down. Hege had long since grown tired of asking him to give up this irritating habit.

Mattis went on: "But you're not only like lightning with eight petaled roses, it's the same with everything you do."

She waved him aside: "Yes, yes, I know." Mattis was satisfied and said no more.

It was using the word lightning that he found so tempting. Strange lines seemed to form inside his head when he used it, and he felt himself drawn toward it. He was terrified of the lightning in the sky—and he never used the word in hot summer weather when there were heavy clouds. But tonight he was safe. They had had two storms already this spring, with real crashing thunder. As usual, when the storm was at its height Mattis had hidden himself in the privy; for someone had once told him that lightning had never struck such buildings. Mattis wasn't sure whether this applied to the whole world, but where he was at least it had proven blissfully true so far.

"Yes, lightning," he mumbled, half to himself, half to Hege, who was tired of his sudden bragging tonight. But Mattis hadn't finished.

"I mean at thinking, too," he said. At this she looked up quickly, as if frightened; something dangerous had been touched. "That'll do for now," she said and closed the matter abruptly. "What's wrong?" he asked. "Nothing. Just you sit quiet."

Hege managed to suppress whatever was trying to come out. The fact was that the tragedy of her simple brother had haunted her for so long now that whenever Mattis used the word think she jumped as if she'd been stung.

Mattis knew something was wrong, but he associated it with the bad con-science he always had because he didn't work like other people. He rattled off his set piece: "You must find me some work tomorrow. Things can't go on like this."

"Yes," she said, not thinking.

"I can't allow this to go on. I haven't earned anything for— "

"No, it's a long time since you came home with anything," she blurted out, a little carelessly, a little sharply. She regretted it the moment it was said; Mattis was very sensitive to criticism on this point, unless he was doing the criticizing himself.

"You shouldn't say things like that to me," he told her, and there was an odd expression in his face.

She blushed and bent her head. But Mattis went on: "Talk to me like you talk to other people."

"Yes, alright."

Hege kept her head down. Whatever could she do with the impossible? Sometimes she couldn't control herself and it was then her words hurt.

p. 9

When more words are used to say something than are needed to say it, there is usually a reason for it. Writers are exceptional in that they never want to use more words than they need to use in order to express everything they want to express, so when they appear to waste language, it must be either a mistake or a deliberate effect. The rest of us can afford to waste language for no purpose, writers cannot.[1]

"Mattis looked to see if the sky was clear and free of clouds this evening, and it was." Almost everything in this sentence is fat that could be cut away. Why "looked to see," as if either looking or seeing alone wasn't enough to survey a sky? Of course Mattis wants to know if there are clouds "this evening"—could he possibly look to see if there are clouds in the sky tomorrow, or April last year? "And it was" would certainly be eliminated if the sentence were written solely to com-municate the action, as it could have been: "Mattis saw that the sky was clear." Even more concisely: "Mattis saw a clear sky." Even more so: "Mattis saw clear sky."

Why does Vesaas include so much more than the action of the sentence requires? One of the reasons for using more words than are needed is because certain feelings, particularly of eagerness and earnestness, can be communicated through the strategic use of excess. It is natural to overload a sentence if you want it to have in it more than other sentences. And the effect of straining a sentence with a surfeit of words is amplified if the language is simple and economical to begin with, as it is in the opening to *The Birds*. There is a kind of long division at work, applicable not only to *The Birds* but to much of narrative prose: what is written "divided by" the most direct means of expressing the content of what is written. What is left over is the remainder, for which some explanation is needed.

What do we learn from the remainder of Vesaas' opening? We learn exactly what we need to know about Mattis and how his mind works to be able to follow the theory of thinking that unfolds between Mattis and his sister over the rest of the scene. Mattis, we learn, is the kind of person who may look at things but not see them and who, it is safe to guess, at times will see without looking. This is the first sign that Mattis is perhaps simple, that he is slower than others at processing the world around him, but that he also may have one or two of the exceptional powers often granted to the simpletons of literature. Though he may not see everything he looks at, to his credit, Mattis looks *for the purpose of seeing* (he "looked to see"), unlike many who look without caring to see. This yearning of his is an indication of Mattis' earnestness (which in literature is often a noble feature of simplicity): in Mattis' mind, looking is burdened with a keenness to see, and sentences are burdened with a longing to express this keenness.[2] Right away, our heart bleeds a little for Mattis, for we already know that his simplicity means he has even fewer words than non-simple people, which in turn means that his few words may buckle under the weight of his sincerity (as the first sentence nearly does). If something can be filled (sentences, eyes), Mattis tries to fill it with more than it can hold. But not every gaze is designed to see, much as not every sentence is designed to carry the added weight of being sincerely felt to be especially true.

We also learn from the opening that Mattis has his own way of thinking. The novel cannot begin "Mattis saw that the sky was clear" because that is not how Mattis comes to know that the sky is clear. First Mattis looks, then he sees, and then sometime later "it was." There is a lag, a period of buffering. And, since this is not how most people evaluate weather, we can foresee that the spaces between looking, seeing, and understanding make Mattis vulnerable, particularly to falling behind. Our heart bleeds a little more. He is as fragile and unaffected as an infant.

But in Vesaas' sympathetic hands, these intervals between looking and seeing, and between seeing and knowing one has seen, can also become a virtue; they can be spaces in which things can exist that otherwise would have no place to exist. These intervals are a *preserve*, a word I use here in the way a naturalist would—a place that exists to conserve living things whose habitats have disappeared and who cannot survive in the world in its current state. One such thing that could possibly only exist in such spaces is Mattis himself. Mattis' mind—which is organized to create such clearances—is a place suited to preserving him, to allowing him to survive; if Mattis' mind did not exist, where would we ever find Mattis? We wouldn't, for there would be no space in which he could live. Mattis is not so much his entire mind as an occupant of the little spaces of safety and calm between the larger, more unwieldy and dominant operations of the mind that he has little confidence in handling. Mattis exists in these spaces like one who owns a proper home but lives in its walls. The narrow coziness of a mind like his is made all the more stunning when put in contrast with the entire, undivided sky, so big and "free of clouds." What does a mind so small do with a sky so big? Will the sky be a kind of earnestness weighing upon Mattis' mind, much as Mattis' sincerity weighs upon his words, and his need to see bursts his vision?

The sky poses no clear threat to Mattis, so he feels safe in saying to his sister Hege: "You're like lightning." But as soon as he does, "The word sent a cold shiver down his spine, but he felt safe all the same, seeing the sky was perfect." For Mattis, we now discover, Hege is like lightning, and the word lightning is also like lightning. The word and what it denotes are not equivalent (the word does not light up the sky), but the word can make lightning strike *within* Mattis, for lightning is nothing if not a cold, vertical shiver "down his spine." The word *lightning*—whether spoken or thought—creates the object lightning, which in this case strikes Mattis. Like natural lightning, this mental lightning can strike further off or nearer to; it can inflict pain, but it also can deliver the pleasure of safety from possible harm. Just as we are concerned with how language will hold up under Mattis' sincerity, we now grow concerned about Mattis' ability to control the lightning he has in him.

And so it is that there ensues an internal fight within Mattis, between sending down lightning and keeping it in the sky. At first, he restrains himself from turning Hege into lightning *tout court* (he tempers the analogy he drew between Hege and lightning by adding, "With those knitting needles of yours, I mean"). But, directly after, Hege's "knitting needles were flashing" like lightning. At one moment, lightning is stored safely in action; in the next moment, lightning is let loose in simile.

For Mattis, handling his ambivalence toward the lightning within him is not just tantamount to thinking. It is thinking itself. "He was slowly tapping his knee with his middle finger—the way he always did when he was thinking. Up and down, up and down." We may as well go ahead and notice that his body follows the oscillations of his mind, but we shouldn't let a minor pattern distract from what is most remarkable here: Mattis has given lightning to Hege, using her needles as lightning rods. Whereas before, only Mattis could be struck by lightning, now Hege too is a conductor for, and a potential victim of, lightning. It is as if, not knowing exactly what to do with the lightning that so attracts him but that he also greatly fears, he tentatively proposes sharing as a momentary solution to turmoil. "But then I'm really grateful for all you do, Hege." Even more, he has given it to her as a gift, to thank her. In doing this, Mattis risks a great deal. Though the sky above them may be "free of clouds," the skies within Mattis and Hege now have omens of lightning—of dangerous thoughts that are also pleasurable and therefore sources of temptation. And as soon as we have pleasure and danger, we have a way of dividing good thoughts from bad: thoughts that can be kept in the sky without striking are good thoughts; thoughts that cannot be kept in the sky, and may actually strike and deliver unwanted feelings, are bad thoughts.

We do not yet know what control Mattis or Hege have over lightning, but Mattis does imagine a safe place in which to hide from anything over which he has no control:

> They had had two storms already this spring, with real crashing thunder. As usual, when the storm was at its height Mattis had hidden himself in the privy; for someone had once told him that lightning had never struck such buildings. Mattis wasn't sure whether this applied to the whole world, but where he was at least it had proven blissfully true so far.
>
> *p. 10*

Mattis recalls a physical place where he would be safe, which could replace the formerly safe company of his sister Hege, who he has put in danger by thinking. Perhaps more importantly, the safe distinctions that had once given a degree of order to Mattis' inner and outer worlds are falling fast. Consider at how many levels Mattis' world is a confounding of ostensibly separate categories: language is confounded with what it denotes; what is in nature is confounded with what is in his thoughts; the rhythms of thinking are confounded with bodily rhythms; the safety of the privy is confounded with safety from potentially harmful thoughts.

"They had had two storms already this spring, with real crashing thunder." This first mention of *thunder* adds another layer to Vesaas' presentation of a philosophy of thinking. Thunder is of course the partner of lightning; they are always together, though as with Mattis' thinking, there is a delay between them, and they always come in the same order. If lightning is a thought, then thunder is the expression of that thought. First the flash of thought, then the prolonged, vibrating, rumble of the thought in language. It is curious that only thought can strike and harm in the world of *The Birds*; thunder is only a frightening clamor, useful for judging the distance between language and the thought it expresses.

But perhaps we speak too soon in dismissing sound as an after-effect of thought:

> "Yes, lightning," he mumbled, half to himself, half to Hege, who was tired of his sudden bragging tonight. But Mattis hadn't finished.
>   "I mean at thinking, too," he said.
>
> *p. 10*

Instead of speaking the word *lightning*, he mumbles it. He makes the sound of it: the rumbling/mumbling of thunder. And the sound of it (the thunder) calls up the thought (the lightning). But what thought does *thunder* call up? It does not call up, as we expect, lightning itself. It calls up thinking. The mumbling of thunder leads to Mattis' tentatively spoken observation, "I mean at thinking, too," a phrase that, as I hear it, is spoken almost as an after-effect of the sound of the word lightning and the feeling of making the word in the mouth. And thinking is quite literally *electrified* with lightning:

At this she looked up quickly, as if frightened; something dangerous had been touched.

"That'll do for now," she said and closed the matter abruptly.

p. 10

Hege touches the word thinking, and draws away from the electrified term. Thinking has lightning in it now.

With this, we get a fairly complete picture of the elegant structure of ideas around which Vesaas' has organized the opening: a man, Mattis, is simple because of the unusual way in which he thinks and says what he thinks. For Mattis, a word such as lightning is not simply a symbol of that which it denotes; it is the thing itself. Speaking the word *lightning*, or having the thought *lightning*, creates the object lightning. This lightning exists as an object inside of Mattis, but also is effected by, and has an effect upon, the natural world in which he lives, a world that is centered upon Hege. Lightning is a thought that Mattis has from time to time, a thought that exemplifies the logic that governs Mattis' way of thinking and can therefore be used to demonstrate that there is order behind what could be read as a puzzling and opaque conversation between Mattis and Hege.

So lightning is a thought. But what kind of thought is it? Lightning is a thought that is pleasurable when it cannot strike but threatens to strike; its pleasure derives from the temptation to release its power, and in so doing to momentarily control an uncontrollable force. Lightning is also a thought that is terrifying when control over it is lost, and it in fact strikes, bringing with it knowledge that had always been present but had not yet manifested itself (had been a potential, as any sky is a potential for lightning, clouds or no clouds). Lightning is a thought that can strike anywhere, which adds to its allure.

One particular thought is the most dangerous thought of all: the thought of thinking itself. If lightning is thought, then thought is lightning. How so? To speak the word *thought* (or *thinking*) brings the idea of thought (or *thinking*) into existence as an object (much as speaking the word *lightning* brings the object lightning into existence). Since thought has no physical form there is no object that corresponds to the word *thought*. Because *thought* must become an object, *thought* becomes lightning, an object that has all the properties of thought. Thought is just like lightning: held in abeyance it can be a source of pleasure, but allowed to strike it is destructive, terrifying, something to put back in the sky. Hege touched the electrified word-thought-object that is *thought*, and she drew back. It was a dangerous thought (an electrified thought), one that could easily turn into knowing. "Hege managed to suppress whatever was trying to come out. The fact was that the tragedy of her simple brother had haunted her for so long now that whenever Mattis used the word think she jumped as if she'd been stung." Bees sting, but in a pinch so could lightning, particularly if mixing one's metaphors were a way of distancing oneself from a threatening metaphor (thought as a kind of lightning). In this case, though, Mattis, in speaking the word *think*, has struck Hege with lightning. The word *think* is electrified; to speak it is to strike lightning.

And what does one do if lightning has struck, and electrified thinking so it cannot be spoken or thought about? At first, one will try not to think.

> Mattis knew something was wrong, but he associated it with the bad con-science he always had because he didn't work like other people. He rattled off his set piece: "You must find me some work tomorrow. Things can't go on like this."
>   "Yes," she said, not thinking.
>   "I can't allow this to go on. I haven't earned anything for—"
>
> *p. 10*

Mattis resorts to language that cannot be electrified because it is dead language: dead through repetition and familiarity. Hege too tries to ground thought by "not thinking." Together, they attempt to quiet down thinking, and promptly settle comfortably into unthinking. They want a clear sky: a clear sky holds no lightning (gives no real pleasure), but it also contains no thought (it is free of thought, as the sky is "free of clouds," and so cannot bring bad thoughts). A clear sky is neutral, and we find that a great deal of discussion can be had without raising clouds or bringing down lightning. Here, "not thinking" does not mean absentmindedly or rashly or stupidly. It means that it is not a phrase of lightning.

It is impossible to keep lightning in a sky that wishes to expel it. And Hege, despite a wish to hold back the lightning Mattis imbued in her, looses it, striking Mattis with her own lightning.

> "No, it's a long time since you came home with anything," she blurted out, a little carelessly, a little sharply. She regretted it the moment it was said; Mattis was very sensitive to criticism on this point, unless he was doing the criticizing himself."
>
> *p. 11*

The double, inverted ironies are clear enough: Mattis has the thought that he has no thought (his mind is defective), and this thought strikes Hege (but does not strike Mattis, except as a general desire to protect Hege); Hege has the thought that Mattis' no-thought (the empty promise of finding work, which is beyond his emotional and intellectual capabilities) should not be treated as proper thought, and this thought strikes Mattis (but does not strike Hege, except for as a general desire to protect Mattis). The clear natural sky is the inverse of the charged inner-sky. The word *thought* has within it the word *lightning*, which has within it the powers of natural lightning.

In this unfolding and development of a theory of thinking, illustrated in the conversation of brother and sister, everything finally becomes transparent. The clouds have come out for all to see. Mattis can see the criticisms that are in Hege's mind, and Hege can see the shame and hurt that are in Mattis' mind. We are sometimes quick to believe that laying our cards on the table openly is a path to growth. Turn the unknown, or unthought, into the known and the thought, and in so doing we will learn more about ourselves and each other, and find some path to resolving the conflicts we have with ourselves and with others. And this is frequently true. But there are occasions, such as this one, in which impenetrability (what I have elsewhere called mystery) is the means by which the type of knowledge that is most needed between Mattis and Hege in this moment can come into being. "'You shouldn't say things like that to me,' he told her, and there was an odd expression in his face" (p. 11). It would be easy to think that Mattis is here communicating a thought to Hege, and that that thought is what produces in Hege an awareness of things that she had not been aware of before.

However, I do not think this is the case. It isn't what Mattis says that effects change in Hege, but a combination of two mysteries: the "odd expression" on Mattis' face and what Mattis exactly means by "things like that." What Mattis says is, at least ethically, quite clear. He is saying: don't hurt me, don't treat me cruelly. But what stops Hege short, makes her blush and lower her head, is that Mattis is no longer "readable." What is this "odd expression"? What can be inferred from it about the contents of Mattis' mind? Whereas Mattis had before been transparent, now he is opaque, armed with a power to evoke a broader claim for himself as a human being than he had before. The mystery of Mattis and Hege had been growing ever thinner as, one after the other, the operations of their minds were laid bare and organized into a system. At the moment when mystery was about to run out (all was to be known), the unknown is replenished, but in such a way that it adds to Vesaas' conception of thinking rather than detracting from it.

In becoming mysterious and opaque, Mattis creates a mind of his own. He is no longer burdened by sincerity, or by a desire to see what is before him. He sees everything that is before him and is now able to speak without waste, "You shouldn't say things like that to me." Nothing can be removed from this admonishment. In becoming unknown to Hege, Mattis becomes known to himself, and in turn finds a language that can express all that he wants to say. Perhaps becoming opaque is a necessary part of the process by which any human being creates a mind of his own.

And when Mattis has, for the moment at least, a mind of his own, he uses it. "She blushed and bent her head. But Mattis went on: 'Talk to me like you talk to other people'" (p. 11). What a command this is! Suddenly, other people exist, not just Mattis and Hege living at the end of a world too wide to consider. And though it is a simple command, it is of the greatest ethical importance. It could be an iron rule: talk to each person as you would talk to other people. Don't talk down to them, or up at them, or as if you have special access to their thoughts. If one breaks this iron rule, it seems that any honest communication becomes impossible. And it is an admonishment that is no doubt in the minds of many, but is quite rarely voiced.

Hege agrees. What she said to Mattis *was* wrong; it was not how she speaks to other people; she had developed a special (and oftentimes, dead) language just for Mattis. The rebuke is so potent that it turns Hege into a blushing head: she too is now opaque. All alone, she must have the thought that Mattis has struck her with; she can no longer allow the logic of the scene to think for her, as it had been. With her "head down" she must answer a very difficult, very human question: "Whatever could she do with the impossible?" Whoever would have guessed at the beginning of the scene that by the end of it we would be asking questions of such gravity? It is as if electricity has coursed through these few dozen snaking sentences to light up the bulb of the entire scene in its final few words.

What do we do with the impossible? Mattis has every right to be spoken to as others are spoken to, but for him to understand in the way others understand is not possible. To speak to Mattis as he would like to be spoken to is, for Hege, ridiculous, something that—for emotional as well as practical reasons—she cannot conceive of doing. Would it destroy Mattis? Humiliate him? Seal him off from her permanently, so that she could not continue to keep him alive—emotionally as well as financially—as she had been doing for so long? It is impossible during the normal course of matters to have an answer to such questions or to risk calamity by trying to do the impossible. Furthermore, as Hege herself knows, "sometimes she couldn't control herself." To try to keep inside oneself what demands to come out is like trying to keep the lightning up in the sky: pointless and absurd. So what does one do about what one cannot control? And how awful it would be for Hege to be alone in her own head, by herself and without Mattis, for the first time in a very long time—as unthinkable as a mother not having her own child somewhere in her head for the whole rest of her life. For Hege, thinking for Mattis was a kind of solution to the problem of thinking for herself.

What do we do with the impossible? One answer is that we speak about it the way we speak about other things. Not as some grand abstraction, but as yet another difficulty we'll have to manage. In doing this, we reclaim it as something human. A second answer, again drawn from what I see in the text, is that we use the impossible as a source of mystery. We use it to break the electrified chain of logic and certainty that endangers us by making us fully known and therefore not ourselves, not human. Beyond this, there may be nothing to do with the impossible but hope it stays in the sky.

Notes

1 See the previous chapter for a discussion of the pressure that content can apply to the expressive capacity of language. Mattis' way of seeing, in so far as it is predicated on the overburdening of language, is reminiscent of a lyricism common to expressions of loss. Further, one can find in Mattis elements of the mystery of looking and the mystery of thinking, which I discussed in the chapter "The Risk of True Confession."
2 See the earlier chapter "The Risk of True Confession" for further discussion of what I refer to there as "the mystery of looking" and "the mystery of thinking."

6

REFLECTIONS ON THE PREVIOUS CHAPTER

In the previous chapter, I closely read the opening to Tarjei Vesaas' *The Birds* ([1957]2016). I tried to show that Vesaas has created not so much a rendering of reality as a rendering of a philosophy, and a fine and rigorous one at that.[1] The passage is as good as a philosophy, which is a sure indication that we should not think of literature as holding a mirror up to the world but as creating a World, one that lives out a philosophy and abides by the rules that apply to that World. This is one reason why there is no need for a fictional character to resemble the people of our world in order to be "believable"; a character only needs to be a creation from which can be inferred his position within a philosophy—a governing set of rules and order—that is true within the world of the work itself. What does Mattis look like, or Hege? What do they smell like, what clothes do they wear, how far from each other do they sit? Does loose change jingle in their pockets when they walk? We don't know, because knowing these things is superfluous to the function of the book's opening scene, which is to bring into being a World from which the rules of this particular World can be divined and considered. If Mattis and Hege were like people you or I might run into, we would have to know more about them to be convinced by them. We do not need more convincing. Mattis and Hege are ideas being lived out (rounded out uncontrollably by the uncontrollable complexity of Vesaas' World), not people we know from our senses. "Truth is the most satisfying relations of the intelligible. Beauty is beheld by the imagination which is appeased by the most satisfying relations of the intelligible" (1922, p. 243), writes James Joyce. The order and sophistication, and obvious beauty, of the rules of thinking that govern the opening to *The Birds* support Joyce's supposition.

Though Vesaas' philosophy is a complex one, we can review its main points quickly. A word (in this case the word *lightning*) brings into being the object *lightning*; this object can be expelled by one person and introjected into another;

the word-object becomes a bizarre object, persecutory even; the pressure of these word-objects are among several important catalysts for thinking, or the avoidance of thinking; the ability to think is predicated on a capacity for one's senses and for language to hold or contain all that one needs them to contain at any given moment. For any reader conversant with Klein and Bion, this description will likely recall the work of these psychoanalysts. It would not be difficult to convert the reading I gave into a discussion of object relations, of container/contained, of splitting and projective identification, and so on. Read with a mind for Klein and Bion, the text may even appear to call out for their famous terms.

So why did I read the text without recourse to Klein and Bion? I have already suggested the first reason: Vesaas' writing is already a theory of thinking (as well as, of course, much more than a theory of thinking), so there is no need to attribute to Bion what is in fact original to Vesaas. If we were to apply Bion to Vesaas we would no doubt lose not only what is unique to Vesaas' but also the suggestiveness and mystery that are central to the vitality of any literary event. Applying Bion converts the mystery that is central to Vesaas' theory into a known—something predicted by Bion beforehand. We see now why it is critically important to understand that literature is not necessarily a rendering of reality: if it were, then we could very well argue that life is just as Vesaas describes, and so the fact that Bion's theory of thinking is roughly expressed in Vesaas' rendering of life is evidence that what Bion says about thinking is empirically true. But, as I have shown, Vesaas' fiction is not a proper measure for the empirical truth of psychological theories.

The second reason I did not apply Bion in my reading is that to do so would be to confuse what is in fact in Vesaas' writing with the memory of Bion that I brought to my reading of Vesaas. Suppose that one had read Bion extensively, then read Vesaas: one would no doubt confuse the theory of thinking expressed by the text with a less mysterious, and therefore more concrete and manageable, memory we have of a theory of thinking (Bion's) that holds some similarities to Vesaas' theory. This happens all the time: a critic attributes to the text something that is really a memory the critic has of an idea from outside of the text. When one finds the depressive position, for example, in a literary event, one is no doubt attributing to the text a memory one has of a concept that the text reminds one of but that is unnecessary to the text. In some instances, it is true, a text will intentionally call out for an idea the reader likely has in his head, provoking the reader to bring their memory into their experience and understanding of the text. But these occasions are uncommon, and, more often than not, the invocation is meant to be ironic; or to bait the reader into becoming more self-conscious about how history and ideology nose their way into readings; or to make light of a reader's inability to understand the problems with applying ideas from memory.

There is a scene in Don DeLillo's *White Noise* (1985) where two professor friends drive out to visit a nearby tourist attraction known as the most photographed barn in America. Still miles out from the barn itself, the signs begin to appear: "THE MOST PHOTOGRAPHED BARN IN AMERICA" (p. 12). They count five of them before reaching the barn itself. There, they mill around as visitors snap pictures of the barn.

> We walked along a cowpath to the slightly elevated spot set aside for viewing and photographing. All the people had cameras; some had tripods, telephoto lenses, filter kits. A man in a booth sold postcards and slides—pictures of the barn taken from the elevated spot.
>
> *p. 12*

The professors don't have cameras themselves, so they watch in silence, until one of them, Murray, expresses what they are both feeling: "'No one sees the barn,' he said finally. A long silence followed. 'Once you've seen the signs about the barn, it becomes impossible to see the barn'" (p. 12). Murray falls into DeLillo's favored kind of mythopoetic waxing on Americana: "'They are taking pictures of taking pictures.'" Then DeLillo finally gets us to the heart of the matter: "'What was the barn like before it was photographed?' he asked. 'What did it look like, how was it different from other barns, how was it similar to other barns?'" (p. 13).

When I write about literature, I am trying to see the barn. I do everything I can *not* to fall into the trap of believing that I am seeing the barn when I am only taking pictures of it. If I require a point of comparison, it must be with other barns, the barns that came before it, or exist alongside of it—literary history can and should be consulted. But it must remain a barn, not an attraction. In DeLillo's case, the comedy is in the fact that there is nothing so wonderful about the barn in the first place to make it so widely photographed. People visit not because it is intrinsically worth seeing—there is no clear reason why this barn, as opposed to another one down the road, should charge money for postcards—but because of the myth of the barn and a desire to be a part of the energy of that myth. Everyone is looking just because many people are pointing.

The same is true whenever we try to write something new about a classic, whether it's a canonical work of literature or a seminal essay such as Freud's "Mourning and Melancholia" (1917). We have to pass the signs to it before we get there, and "once you've seen the signs about the barn, it becomes impossible to see the barn." And so the literature surrounding "Mourning and Melancholia" becomes like those snapping photographers, who aren't really reading the text so much as "taking pictures of taking pictures"—they're saying they've been there, not to the barn so much as to the vantage point from which all other visitors collectively make the barn famous. They are part of the barn's fame. Their attention no longer has anything to do with barns; it wholly ignores what the barn is as a barn, and does nothing with the barn but add another votive to its altar. The lesson is massive: we should read Vesaas as if it had never been "photographed" before—as if we had no Bionian or Kleinian telephoto lens through which to snap yet another picture. This gives us a snowflake's chance in hell—certainly no guarantee: it may be that no one will ever see the ceiling of the Sistine Chapel again—of really seeing the barn, of really reading Vesaas.

As DeLillo tells it, we have no choice but to read the signs before we get to the attraction. We would never go there in the first place if it weren't for the picture-taking crowds. And this is true for any serious reading. Perhaps I can avoid reading the criticism surrounding a particular text or author,[2] but I may, by happenstance, have read a lot of Bion or all of Klein and then, by a stroke of chance, picked up *The Birds* and opened to page one. There is nothing I can do about what I've just read and its relation to what I now by chance am reading. And in such circumstances, how can I not want to say that Mattis' relationship to lightning is not Bionian in this sense? It's difficult to resist pointing out that when Mattis gives lightning to Hege it resembles projective identification. More broadly, what do I do with my memory of Bion when reading Vesaas?—which is like asking, what do I do with my memory of the signs for the world's most photographed barn if I want to see the barn, as opposed to merely look in its direction?

This question of what to do with knowledge is a question not just for critics but also for fiction writers. Though little has been written on the subject, I find that how a writer handles his or her own erudition has considerable influence on their style and reputation. Erudition exerts a tremendous pressure on style, and one must manage that pressure carefully. For James Joyce, erudition was central to his legend, and is everywhere in his aesthetic. In *A Portrait of the Artist as a Young Man* (1922), we have such statements as, "He thought himself into confidence" (p. 74) and "By thinking of things you could understand them" (p. 45). This is a powerful life philosophy, based on the idea of accumulation and comprehension, a world built of mental life and the presumption that life yields to study and observation. This is precisely the precept that writers like Paul Bowles and Malcolm Lowry would challenge in the 1940s and that was utterly closed down by Samuel Beckett. In Beckett, one does not think oneself into confidence; one speaks to stave off thinking, and speaks in the hope of stumbling on something that one recognizes as meaning or significance.

For other writers, erudition must be kept out of style. It isn't a part of the legend. Though logically we know that Hemingway must have been nearly as much of a know-it-all as Joyce, we don't talk so often about Hemingway's brain-power, or trade stories of his intellectual feats as is commonly done with Joyce,[3] because Hemingway's style is decidedly unlearned. Like so many American writers of his generation, he is a little rough around the edges, smart as opposed to edu-cated, sensual as opposed to sentimental, an outsider as opposed to an insider, lost, detached. Hemingway wasn't for making the reader feel stupid or in awe of his erudition. Joyce was. Hemingway could have set out to dazzle in this way, but there was no place for that in his style, or in the self-image and ideology that were carried in that style.

This is all to say that decisions must be made all the time about what to do with what we know when faced with the task of understanding a thing for what it is.

The problem, as I see it, is that it is too easy to attribute to the text something that ought to be attributed to the critic's own memory. Very often, critics speak as if something—the depressive position, the unconscious, transference-counter-transference—is actually in the text, when the truth is that it is in the critic's mind. These terms are not presented as what they really are: things the reader already knows that he can use to replace the endless suggestiveness and unique reality of literature with a more manageable form. A critic must understand that his memory of Bion is not a part of the text, but a part of what he cannot help but bring to his reading, and he must handle it with the same care that Hemingway and Joyce bring to the matter of where and if to include all they know about literary history in their own writing. As with so many things, this will all be done through choices about, and the development of, an individual critical style.

Moreover, as we gather again from Hemingway and Joyce, how much erudition one includes in one's criticism will not necessarily determine the quality of that criticism. It will merely create two different kinds of criticism. Erudition is not so much a matter of how much helpful knowledge can be conveyed to the reader (erudition is as likely to confuse or bore the reader as it is to enlighten him) but a matter of the style the critic wants to create. We learn as much from reading Hemingway as we do from reading Joyce[4]; the same is true of critics as different as Harold Bloom and William H. Gass. If we look back to Mattis and Hege, we can say that being simple is neither a disadvantage nor an advantage, just different. It is all in the execution. A simple style can be all-knowing and precious and an erudite style mundane and flat. A simple style can still communicate hearty chunks of information, and an erudite style can still, when necessary, be pointed and unadorned.

Nonetheless, erudition that is a hurricane of facts and names and terms and theories and footnotes is also a hurricane of language that is rigid in memory. It is the "tripods, telephoto lenses, filter kits" of literary criticism. It is expensive equipment for seeing better. Though, as we know, the equipment cannot help us see better *until* we have actually seen the barn. And of course if you bring a tripod along with you, you'll use it. Mattis tells Hege, "Talk to me like you talk to other people." This does not mean that Hege must forget everything she once knew about Mattis. It means that to communicate with him Hege must put aside equipment. A style created in the moment, not from memory, will be a style whose *language* (though not all of the knowledge expressed in that language) only comes from the barn and its surroundings. This is again a matter of attribution: knowing what is the barn, and knowing what is the memory of the barn, and also knowing what is the meaning of all the equipment and people surrounding the barn.

James Joyce again:

> We are right, he said, and the others are wrong. To speak of these things and to try to understand their nature and, having understood it, to try slowly and humbly and constantly to express, to press out again, from the gross earth or what it brings forth, from sound and shape and colour which

are the prison gates of our soul, an image of the beauty we have come to understand—that is art.

p. 242

When Joyce speaks of "the gross earth and what it brings forth" he is speaking of natural language and all the ways it can surprise us with what it produces. If there is a case to be made for what I have been calling a simple style, this would be it: the more we force ourselves to make use of the gross earth the more it will bring forth its natural riches. There is something about this kind of farm-to-table criticism that is appropriate for talking about a thing like a barn.

In my own reading of Versaas, I felt much the same: the work called out for a certain kind of reading. Maybe I would not have seen what I did in Versaas if I had not read Bion, but I had to forget the language of Bion in order to write in a style in which I could "slowly and humbly and constantly" express not only what the text wanted heard ("talk to me like you talk to other people") but what it wanted considered but not understood (what do we do with the impossible?). Franz Kafka once bemoaned:

> I can't explain to you or anybody else what it's like inside me. How could I begin to explain; I can't even explain to myself. But even this is not the main thing; the main thing is obvious: it is impossible to live like a human being around me; you see this and yet you don't want to believe it?

1990, p. 221

Here we get the contradictions of art: art is a barn, it can't explain what it is, so it calls out to be seen for what it is. Yet, no matter how often it asks to be understood on its own terms we continue to take pictures of it. We are aware of this, but we don't want to believe it. The question is: why do we continue picture taking?

Notes

1 I am particularly indebted to the ideas of William H. Gass in this chapter, as Gass beautifully and rigorously explores the philosophical cohesion on which much fiction rests in *Fiction and the Figures of Life* (1979). In so far as this chapter considers the relationship of literature to the philosophy of psychology, it also calls to mind issues that have been explored by Jonathan Lear in *Open Minded* (1999) and *Wisdom Won From Illness* (2017).

2 I am by no means saying one ought to do this, just that it is possible to read a text without consulting the critical literature around it.

3 Practically the first thing one learns upon walking into the Joyce Museum in Dublin is that Joyce knew 16 languages and he taught himself Norwegian in three weeks so he could read Ibsen in the original.

4 Though if you want to learn certain facts about the Catholic liturgy you would get more from Joyce: his erudition is packaged as arcane but impressive data.

7

WHAT IS A DREAM AND HOW DO YOU WRITE ONE?

For each human experience, there seems to be at least one work of literature that has captured what it is like to have, or to have had, or to be having that experience. This is because great literature is often, though not always, a recreation of life in language so much like life that the reader feels the writer has captured what it is like to live through all that human beings are capable of living through, and much that they cannot live through but can envision. Whether it be acute pain and agony, the touch of an affectionate finger, or the thoughts and feelings of the human mind as it thinks and feels, writers have depicted it so that readers find what they read to be very much like life as they know life to be. Some depictions are abstract, others photogenic, but one way or another literature must be able to make us say, of almost every conceivable event and circumstance: life is like that.

The only exception to this rule that I know of is dreams. "Tell a dream, lose a reader," (Qtd. in Amis, 2001, p. 446) cautioned Henry James. And here is Nathaniel Hawthorne expressing a related frustration, in a notebook entry of 1842:

> To write a dream, which shall resemble the real course of a dream, with all its inconsistency, its eccentricity and aimlessness—with nevertheless a leading idea running through the whole. Up to this old age of the world, no such thing has ever been written.
>
> *1932, p. 99*

Francine Prose, struck by the "timidity" of a dream scene she included in a draft of her novel, describes cutting the dream out because it reads not as a dream, but as a mannered way of relating what a character thinks: "I'd realized that the dream in my novel didn't sound like a dream but rather like a novelist's attempt to signal that a character knows more about the present—and the future—than he realizes" (2013). Dreams in literature most often strike the reader as false and unconvincing, a pale and provisional version of the real thing. A dream in a novel does not have what Vladimir Nabokov called the "quiver and shimmer" (1981, p. 56) of actual dreaming. What is more, often a dream in literature is not, really, a dream at all; rather, as Prose realized of her own attempt at fictionalizing a dream, it is a device for getting to the reader information that has no natural place in the reality that the work describes. A dream forebodes; it reveals forbidden wishes; it supplies motives for actions that otherwise would seem unprompted. It is a handy shortcut for a writer in a squeeze, but it is not dreaming as we know it.

Why would this be? What is it about dreams, more than anything else that human beings feel and undergo, that makes writing them so difficult? To begin with, dreams may be difficult to write because they are, from a writer's standpoint, more challenging than life in every way. By this I mean that the demand placed on language to express a dream element is always greater than the demand placed on language to express the equivalent element in reality. A dream lettuce is more difficult to write than a real lettuce. It is never the case, as far as I can tell, that a dream *reduces* the burden on a writer. Something must be done to language by the writer so that it can represent dreams that does not have to be done to language to represent reality; whatever this *something* is, it strains language. This raises the possibility that language was not developed with dreams in mind. Further adding to this burden, what happens in dreams is frequently bizarre, chaotic, irrational, and contrary to much of what gives reality its "realness." It is hard enough to describe a lettuce, let alone a dream lettuce, let alone a dream lettuce that barks like a dog. Perhaps dreaming places more of a burden on the expressive capacities of language than language can hold up against.

But this shouldn't be, for poetic language has never had any difficulty with the surreal, the fantastic, the phantasmagoric, all of which are rife with dream-like elements. The impossible has not tended to ring untrue in literature, at least not in the hands of the best writers. Look how, in the opening of "A Very Old Man with Enormous Wings" (1972), Gabriel García Márquez gives to the reader a world in which its fantastic qualities are its most vividly real:

> On the third day of rain they had killed so many crabs inside the house that Pelayo had to cross his drenched courtyard and throw them into the sea, because the newborn child had a temperature all night and they thought it was due to the stench. The world had been sad since Tuesday. Sea and sky were a single ash-gray thing and the sands of the beach, which on March nights glimmered like powdered light, had become a stew of mud and rotten shellfish. The light was so weak at noon that when Pelayo was coming back to the house after throwing away the crabs, it was hard for him to see what it was that was moving and groaning in the rear of the courtyard. He had to go very close to see that it was an old man, a very old man, lying face down in the mud, who, in spite of his tremendous efforts, couldn't get up, impeded by his enormous wings.

p. 105

This is not a dream, nor is it particularly dream-like. But the scene does reflect the aesthetics of dreams: emotions are attributed not to individuals, but to the world itself; the ether grows fuzzy, vaguely somber; we are both in a time and place and outside of time and place, as in a bedtime story; an old man has the wings of an angel. But none of these dream-like qualities make the scene feel like fakery. The reader is not in any way prevented from believing in this strange world to the extent the reader must believe in it to draw pleasure from it as literature. The same cannot usually be said of dreams and dreaming when they appear in literature, even when the content in both cases is equally strange or absurd. Something about dreams niggles the reader in a way that the merely fantastic does not.

In fact, from a certain vantage point, language is not only capable of depicting the irrational and bizarre content of dreams but is extraordinarily well suited to representing the specific processes that make dreams so peculiar: condensation, displacement, indirect representation, symbolization, and so forth. As Lacan suggested, it is possible to think of the unconscious as having the structure of a language. If this is so, metonymy and metaphor are linguistic analogues to the psychological functions of displacement and condensation. While this may be true, practically speaking I think we can go further than Lacan and say that language was made for dreaming. Literary language sets itself apart largely by its use of metaphor and metonymy, so literature distinguishes itself by its readiness to depict dreams. Metaphor and metonymy are omnipresent across all literature as a means of representing condensation and displacement (Don Quixote's lance, Kafka's giant beetle, the red hunting cap worn by Holden Caufield); accordingly, literature is not only capable of representing the oddities of dreams, it is positively born to serve this function. If this is so, dreams in literature do not fall flat because language doesn't have what it takes to depict them.

However, the very idea that language is well suited to depicting the manifest content of dreams may rest on the presumption that images in dreams are observed much like images in reality; hence, depicting images as seen in dreams is akin to depicting objects as seen in reality. A dream may be representable in language because a dream, in the experience of the dreamer, is a perception—if we see, for example, a horse in a dream we see it *perceptively* in the same way we would perceive a horse in reality. If, to take another example, I tell of seeing a cat race across a narrow ledge, I am describing what I perceived. If I tell of a dream in which a cat raced across a narrow ledge, I am also describing what I perceived. Though there may be any number of qualities that differentiate the dream from the real event, and though there are powerful feelings in dreams that may indicate presences in a way that is unique to dreams, in both cases much of what I would say *was* the dream was an observing of a physical world. This being so can be seen as a pre-condition for any possibility of depicting dreams in language. Dream scenes must be "tellable," whether to a reader or an analyst, in a way that shares something fundamental with the "tellable" aspects of reality.

But the challenge to the writer who wants to write a dream would be even greater if one does not in fact perceive dreams in the way one feels one does. Is it true that when we see a horse, for example, in a dream, we see it in the same sense that we see an identical horse in reality? If we do not, depicting a dream horse in language in the same way we would depict a real horse in language would lead to a misrepresentation, which could be the reason why dreams in literature seem fabricated. At a basic level, we are wrong to say we "see" dreams because our eyes are closed when we dream; we cannot see a dream image in the same way that we see the physical world. Gilbert Ryle has said that:

> to see is one thing; to picture or visualize is another … When a person says that he 'sees' something which he is not seeing, he knows that what he is doing is something which is *totally different* in *kind* from seeing.
>
> *p. 246*

But if I "see" a cat running across a ledge in a dream, what am I doing if I am not "seeing"?

In *Imagination* (1936) and *The Psychology of Imagination* (1940), Jean-Paul Sartre tries to answer this question. For Sartre, perceptions are different from the images we hold of something in our mind because when we perceive an object we can only see one part of it at any given time, whereas if we form an image of an object in our mind we can "perceive" all parts of the object at once. I can only perceive one side of a horse at a single moment, but if I have the image of a horse I can see every side of the horse simultaneously. This is the reason why we do not confuse perceived objects with imagined objects: the two have, as Sartre points out in *Imagination*, an "identity of essence" (p. 2) (they appear the same), but not an "identity of existence" (p. 2) (they are of different kinds). Imagining, as Edward S. Casey has noted, "has no such basis in observation; at most, it can be said to be 'quasi-observational,' that is, to induce in the imaginer a sense of observing when he is in fact not observing at all" (1981, p. 144). This seems critical to the difficulty of describing dreams, apart even from the problem of what a dream is like: a dream is quasi-observational, in that it induces in the imaginer a sense of observing when he is in fact not observing. If this conception of observation is overlooked by an author, the quality of a depiction of a dream could fall apart, since a dream is depicted as perceived, rather than imagined in the Sartrean sense.

Great writers have recognized this and tried with some success to alter their depictions of dreams to account for it. Here is Vladimir Nabokov's description of a dream he had about butterflies:

> 23 NOV 1964, 6:45 A.M.: End of a long "butterfly" dream which started after I had fallen asleep following upon a sterile awakening at 6:15 A.M. Have arrived (by funicular?) at a collecting ground of timberland (in Switzerland? In Spain?), but in order to get to it have to cross the hall of a large gay hotel. Very spry and thin, dressed in white, skip down the steps on the other side and find myself on the marshy border of a lake. Lots of bog flowers, rich soil, colorful, sunny, but not one single butterfly (familiar sensation in dream).

Instead of a net, am carrying a huge spoon—cannot understand how I managed to forget my net and bring this thing—wonder how I shall catch anything with it. Notice a kind of letter box open on the right side, full of butterflies somebody has collected and left there. One is alive—a marvelous aberration of the Green Fritillary, with unusually elongated wings, the green all fused together and the brown of an extraordinary variegated hue. It eyes me in conscious agony as I try to kill it by pinching its thick thorax—very tenacious of life. Finally slip it into a morocco case—old, red, zippered. Then realize that all the time a man camouflaged in some way is seated next to me, to the left, in front of the receptacle in which the butterflies are, and prepares a slide for the microscope. We converse in English. He is the owner of the butterflies. I am very much embarrassed. Offer to return the Fritillary. He declines with polite halfheartedness.

p. 86

A writer must adapt stylistically to depict a dream in such a way that the dream is both perceived in the way that reality is perceived and not perceived that way at all. Nabokov tries to accomplish this by removing the "I" pronoun as often as he can. He writes, "Instead of a net, carrying a huge spoon," rather than "Instead of a net, I am carrying a huge spoon"; "Wonder how I shall catch anything with it," not "I wonder how I shall catch anything with it"; "I notice a kind of letter box" has been reformed into "Notice a kind of letter box." Nabokov uses a surprisingly facile stylistic technique to capture the feeling of a dream. The idea underlying this technique seems to be that, in dreams, an "I" is not always felt to be perceiving or responding to the dream event; it is as if one is witnessing the dream, but not from a single perspective, or perhaps the "I" that is watching the dream is different from the "I" that is awake. It feels wrong to say, "I am looking at the dream"; more accurate to say, "the dream is being experienced," with the agentless passive voice posing the critical question: experienced by whom? Nabokov also underscores the difference between a perceived phenomenon and an imagined image in the way he depicts the Green Fritillary; certainly, the Green Fritillary is not a butterfly Nabokov sees in the dream and then describes, but a type of butterfly that he knows already very well. He is not studying it, but presenting the characteristics typical of the species: "elongated wings," "thick thorax." These anatomical details come from Nabokov's life-long study of butterflies, not from empirical study in the moment. He knows these things about the Green Fritillary from years of work as a lepidopterist; he doesn't see these things about it during the dream. The combination of these two stylistic tricks elevates the Green Fritillary, in its reality and in the dreamer's relationship to it, above the rest of the scenery, which merely washes crudely over his mind's eye.

The challenge to the writer, then, is that literature cannot hold a mirror up to dreams or reality in any straightforward way. If we imagine that a dream holds up a mirror (however distorted) to reality and that the writer depicts the dream by holding a mirror up to the dream, then we are on a fool's errand: a dream is not perceived in the way life is, and any representation is bound to fall short of its object. In *Sylvie and Bruno Concluded,* Lewis Carroll whimsically pokes fun at any presumption that a representation could, or should, attempt to equal the object it is meant to represent:

> "What a useful thing a pocket-map is!" I remarked.
>
> "That's another thing we've learned from your Nation," said Mein Herr, "map-making. But we've carried it much further than you. What do *you* consider the *largest* map that would be really useful?"
>
> "About six inches to the mile."
>
> "Only *six inches!*" exclaimed Mein Herr. "We very soon got to six yards to the mile. Then we tried a *hundred* yard to the mile. And then came the grandest idea of all! We actually made a map of the country, on the scale of a *mile to the mile!*"
>
> "Have you used it much?" I enquired.
>
> "It has never been spread out, yet," said Mein Herr: "the farmers objected: they said it would cover the whole country, and shut out the sunlight! So we now use the country itself, as its own map, and I assure you it does nearly as well."
>
> *p. 137*

The Argentine poet and essayist Jorge Luis Borges imagines much the same thing in his parable, "On Exactitude in Science" (1998), though Borges casts an entirely different mood from Carroll:

> In that Empire, the Art of Cartography attained such Perfection that the map of a single Province occupied the entirety of a City, and the map of the Empire, the entirety of a Province. In time, those Unconscionable Maps no longer satisfied, and the Cartographers Guilds stuck a Map of the Empire whose size was that of the Empire, and which coincided point for point with it. The following Generations, who were now so fond of the Study of Cartography as their Forebears had been, saw that that vast map was Useless, and not without some Pitilessness was it, that they delivered it up to the Inclemencies of Sun and Winters. In the Deserts of the West, still today, there are Tattered Ruins of that Map, inhabited by Animals and Beggars; in all the Land there is no other Relic of the Disciplines of Geography.
>
> *p. 325*

For Borges, literature that measures itself by its ability to mirror life is "Useless" because, even in its most ambitious form, it only creates what was there already, and because much of what literature depicts has no physical form and is infinite in scale. The Empire, however vast, is bounded, and its map is also bounded; the Cartographers are able to create a map of it because they have a bounded entity to map. But life is infinite, and how to create a map of the infinite? How does one represent something like a dream, which is not bounded, not even empirically observed in the traditional sense? To create a map of Infinity is a special project, one that interests Borges, for it is both absurd and fantastical in just the way Borges imagines the world. It is also central to the absurdity of trying to depict a dream—any such map would have to be infinitely large, and a map of infinite proportions could serve no practical purpose, and would be no different from what it represented.

Much as Nabokov tried to modify his style to reflect the quasi-observational way dreams are perceived, Borges intentionally writes dreams in a way that minimizes what is observationally important about them, and puts all observations in the service of representing the *concept* of a dream. Borges depicts everything that is perceived in a dream as secondary to, and illustrative of, the very idea of a dream itself. This is his way of accomplishing what the Cartographers had not: a viable map of the Infinite. In Borges' "A Dream" (2009), what is dreamt is nothing but the very nature of dreaming itself—a dream of a dream:

> In a deserted place in Iran there is a not very tall stone tower that has neither door nor window. In the only room (with a dirt floor and shaped like a circle) there is a wooden table and a bench. In that circular cell, a man who looks like me is writing in letters I cannot understand a long poem about a man who in another circular cell … The process never ends and no one will be able to read what the prisoners write.

If man is both dreamer and dreamed, there is a regression of dreaming to infinity in which each person is trapped. The upshot is that our lives are spent in search of an Unmoved Dreamer on which the infinite chain of dreaming is dependent; we try to wake up by finding a figure who is not the object of another's dream, though we would have to travel an infinite distance to find such a person. Consequently, writing a dream is wrong-headed from the very start because all writing is a depiction of a dream masquerading as a depiction of reality. In writing dreams in this way, Borges shirks the most acute difficulties of depicting dreams by making what is observable in the dream a means of depicting the conceptual, and by eliminating any meaningful distinction between dream and reality.

However, in a different work, Borges suggests that dreams may be difficult to write because dreams are, by their very essence, *of another planet*. Here is his poem "The Dream" (1999):

> If dreaming's (as they say) a respite,
> a simple distraction of the mind,
> why is it, if abruptly you wake from one,
> you feel you've been robbed?
> Why's rising too soon so sad?
> Time takes from us an unthinkable gift,
> one so intimate it's only translatable
> in an unconsciousness the night gilds
> with dreams that may well be cut-off

reflections of the treasures of the darkness,
from a timeless, nameless orb
that the day distorts in its mirrors.
Who will you be tonight in the dark dream,
From the other side of the wall?

Borges is here directing us to the fact that the world of dreams often feels separated from us very much in the way that other planets and moons feel separate from us. This is not an idle metaphor. It is an attempt to draw a line between feelings that human beings have about the existence of other planets and the feelings humans have about dreams, particularly their own. As Borges presents it, the situation is this: when sleeping, I am on one side of the wall; when awake I am on the other side. The question is: why should I care what occurs on the far side of the wall if it is on the near side of the wall that I understand myself to be most clearly alive? As I read Borges here, the feeling of *why should I care about the other side of the wall* derives from a primitive sensitivity to those things that are tremendously alive but have nothing to do with us. In fact, they have so little to do with us that in pondering them we can nearly imagine our own irrelevance. Borges pictures the far side of the wall as "a timeless, nameless orb"; quite literally another planet, where life, to our surprise and consternation, goes on without us, much as dreams go on without us whether we remember them or not, try to understand them or not. Children sometimes experience a small dose of this sort of unpleasant surprise when, after missing a day or two of school because of illness, they learn that life at their school apparently goes on much the same without them. It's quite as if the child isn't needed at all.

But Borges goes no further than the conceptual. He does not try to envision this orb in any detail or capture the specific feelings that would make our dreams like distant planets. He is not that kind of writer. Fyodor Dostoevsky, fortunately, has taken the likeness of planets and dreams and made it the centerpiece of his great story, "The Dream of a Ridiculous Man" ([1877]1997). In the story, a man who begins to see life as suffused with the feeling of *it makes no difference* determines to kill himself. For two months "an excellent revolver" sits in a drawer at his home, but on the night of the story, looking up at a little star in the sky, he resolves that he will commit suicide that very night. But then a young girl, sobbing and "terrified by something," tugs at his coat sleeve:

Though she did not speak all the words out, I understood that her mother was dying somewhere, or something had happened with them there, and she has run out to call someone, to find something so as to help her mother. But I did not go with her and, on the contrary suddenly had the idea of chasing her away.

p. 322

The narrator does just that: he shoos her off. Then returns home and recaptures his old suicidal feeling:

> A whole candle burns down overnight. I quietly sat down at the table, took out the revolver, and placed it in front of me. As I placed it there, I remember asking myself: "Is it so?" and answering myself quite affirmatively: "It is." Meaning I would shoot myself. I knew that I would shoot myself that night for certain, but how long I would stay sitting at the table then—that I did not know. And of course I would have shot myself if it hadn't been for that girl.
>
> *p. 323*

It is the girl that brings home to him a question lurking inside the feeling of *it makes no difference*, setting off an investigation into the reason for his attachment to the girl:

> You see: though it made no difference to me, I did still feel pain, for instance. If someone hit me, I would feel pain. The same in the moral respect: if something very pitiful happened, I would feel pity, just as when it still made a difference to me in life. And I felt pity that night: I certainly would have helped a child. Why, then, had I not helped the little girl? From an idea that had come along then: as she was pulling and calling to me, a question suddenly arose before me, and I couldn't resolve it. The question was an idle one, but I got angry. I got angry owing to the conclusion that, if I had already resolved to kill myself that night, it followed that now more than ever everything in the world should make no difference to me. Why, then, did I suddenly feel that it did make a difference, and that I pitied the girl? I remember that I pitied her very much; even to the point of some strange pain, even quite incredible in my situation. Really, I'm unable to express the fleeting feeling I had then any better, but the feeling continued at home as well, when I had already settled at my table, and I was extremely vexed, as I hadn't been for a long time. Reasoning flowed from reasoning. It seemed clear that, if I was a man and not yet a zero, then, as long as I did not turn into a zero, I was alive, and consequently could suffer, be angry and feel shame for my actions. Good. But if I was going to kill myself in two hours, for instance, then what was the girl to me and what did I care then about shame or anything in the world?
>
> *p. 323*

But this reasoning is unsatisfactory, until the narrator lands upon an image that encapsulates his surprise at finding there are limits that can be reached through the feeling of *it makes no difference*. He says:

> I remember that, sitting and reasoning, I turned all these new questions, which came crowding one after another, even in quite a different direction and invented something quite new. For instance, there suddenly came to me a

strange consideration, that if I had once lived on the moon or on Mars, and had committed some most shameful and dishonorable act there, such as can only be imagined, and had been abused and dishonored for it as one can only perhaps feel and imagine in a dream, a nightmare, and if, ending up later on earth, I continued to preserve an awareness of what I had done on the other planet, and knew at the same time that I would never ever return there, then, looking from the earth to the moon—would it *make any difference* to me, or not? Would I feel shame for that act, or not?

p. 324

Though we return to our dreams each night, we cannot know that we will return to the planet where we were the previous night, a planet which we may have many feelings about but tenuous memories. No matter the intensity of the life we led there or the memories we are committed to keeping of that place, once we are no longer there our relevance to that place may be nothing, or feel like nothing, or strike us as unfathomably obscure. Accordingly, there is a feeling about a dream that stands alongside the intensity of dreams, and that is the acute feeling of pondering a place so distant that it is as much a matter of faith as it is observation that it exists; it is a pondering of vast, marvelous irrelevance. And yet on that planet are things that keep us alive, which, though there is nothing in nature to demand that they retain a hold on us, they continue miraculously to have a hold on us. The connection is mystifying; this other planet is extraneous to us, but at the same time it seems to take an interest in us in a way that nothing else on this side of the wall does. It recalls the counterintuitive phenomenon of quantum entanglement, frequently called "spooky action at a distance"; this is when two particles are separated by billions of light years, but nevertheless a change in one particle *instantaneously* results in a change in the other particle. What difference could it make to one particle what occurs to another particle so far away? It could not make a difference, and yet it does, and it is this question that keeps the narrator of Dostoevsky's story from suicide.

What I take from this is that dreams exist regardless of whether they make any difference; this grants them both their wonderful semi-absurdity and the integrity of the messages they send. They do not depend upon their meaningfulness to be as remarkable as they are. In this way, they survive the feeling of *it makes no difference*. And just because dreams are meaningful does not make it any less baffling that they can mean anything to us at all. If they do not have to make any difference to us, then they are granted a life of their own, allowed to be something more than a significant message. They are simultaneously a part of us and apart from us, and that means letting them go on without us, or at times caring little for us, much like children. And just as with children, it is the part of them that goes on without us that makes them interesting.

This apartness, *this independence*, is scarcely invoked by writers in their depictions of dreams and dreaming. In literature, dreams are enormously important, almost immodestly so. It is as if we (reader and writer) are standing on the top of a tall mountain on our planet awaiting transmission from the dream planet, and once we get the transmission nothing could be more urgent than deciphering the message. And it may be important to do this, but it could also be the case that treating dreams this way misrepresents them by taking out of them the very feeling that Dostoevsky says makes them so important: the feeling of *it makes no difference*. Dreams are challenging to write because novels have room only for what is "important," and dreams are associated with deep and profound meanings from the dark. Capturing the aspect of dreams that has to do with caring nothing for what we make of them, or learn from them, is generally given short shrift. We assume that dreams *mean* rather than do something else, something (what?) that might make them seem more real.

Up to this point I have placed all blame on the writer, and on language itself, for the failure to make dreams in fiction authentic. But the blame may fall on readers, or even the act of reading, for turning dreams in literature into mannered tableaux. Consider the following: a dream, if it is to be convincing, must not be recognized as a dream in the moment. To recognize a dream as a dream is to be taken out of the reality of the dream and therefore to be thinking as one who is awake. But a dream is also something from which one eventually awakes—otherwise there can be no recognition of a dream. A dream is something we are fooled by, and then not fooled by. We are under its spell, but from the outset, the spell is wearing off, the moment of awakening draws nearer. There is something in each person that both wants to sleep and dream and wants to leave dreams behind and awaken.

Reading is the best example we have of this process at work. We read a novel because we want to submit to, and contribute our part to, a dream in which we can for stretches of time suspend our disbelief (let our censorious critical faculty stand down); at the same time, reading is always an exercise of our critical mind's capacity to wake up from this dream by noticing ways in which the appearance of the novel masks a submerged meaning or message or view of reality. Both these processes are always present when reading, even in our earliest reading experiences. We could not read uncritically, even if we desired to, for reading entails being only half-fooled, never all-fooled. It demands taking in as much as one can of what is occurring in the language (becoming ourselves the object of the work) and thinking for ourselves in order to fill up the part of the book left open for the reader. We "open" a book because there is space for the reader, and we enter that clearance with the tools with which we enter life: some mixture of intuition and decisive judgment. For Virginia Woolf, as she describes in "How Should One Read a Book?" (1932), this seesawing of submission and critical aggression is what it means to read:

> The first process, to receive impressions with the utmost understanding, is only half the process of reading; it must be completed, if we are to get the whole pleasure from a book, by another. We must pass judgment upon these multitudinous impressions; we must make of these fleeting shapes one that is hard and lasting. But not directly. Wait for the dust of reading to settle; for the

conflict and the questioning to die down; walk, talk, pull the dead petals from a rose, or fall asleep. Then suddenly without our willing it, for it is thus that Nature undertakes these transitions, the book will return, but differently. It will float to the top of the mind as a whole.

p. 241

Woolf goes on, arguing that judgment is an irresistible force that acts against the mysterious and the unknown, which sustain literature:

It would be foolish … to pretend that the second part of reading, to judge, to compare, is as simple as the first—to open the mind wide to the fast flocking of innumerable impressions. To continue reading without the book before you, to hold one shadow-shape against another, to have read widely enough and with enough understanding to make such comparisons alive and illuminating—that is difficult; it is still more difficult to press further and to say, 'Not only is the book of this sort, but it is of this value; here it fails; here it succeeds; this is bad; that is good.' To carry out this part of a reader's duty needs such imagination, insight, and learning that it is hard to conceive of any one mind sufficiently endowed; impossible for the most self-confident to find more than the seeds of such powers in himself. Would it not be wiser, then, to remit this part of reading and to allow the critics, the gowned and furred authorities of the library, to decide the question of the book's absolute value for us? Yet how impossible! We may stress the value of sympathy; we may try to sink our won identity as we read. But we know that we cannot sympathize wholly or immerse ourselves wholly; there is always a demon in us who whispers, 'I hate, I love,' and we cannot silence him.

p. 242

So the critical faculty—which learns from a young age to cast off veils in pursuit of deeper truth and thereby to enter adult life (the awoken world)—is vigilant against the seductions of dreams. It is buoyant; it pulls the reader to the surface and, in doing so, draws a line between dreaming/reading and waking/living. To the degree this is so, it would make sense that depicting dreams convincingly would be difficult: there is something in reading that wants us to awaken. The writer who writes a dream is in the process of creating a reader who, as reader, is possessed of a desire to awaken from the dream to which he has submitted. And as we know, if we want to awaken from a dream, the spell is already half-broken. When Henry James says, "Tell a dream, lose a reader," he is saying that a dream in writing is creating its own destruction in so far as it is trying to convince a reader of something of which he ought not be convinced if he is reading as he should. The better the reader, the more immediate and decisive the attack on a depiction that calls out for an uncritical reader (an anti-reader). And certainly, if a reader knows anything about dreams, he will be on the lookout for what they could mean and for the "unrealness" of their contents, in which case it is natural that the critical faculty would be on its guard against falling prey to the seduction. A dream gets a reader's back up like nothing else.

The reader's critical faculty must, in that case, be dealt with somehow, else it sink every dream, like a pea under a mattress that ruins sleep night after night. But how? It cannot be destroyed; it is an indefatigable demon, and we need it to wake up. And yet the waking up must not so hurry us back to reality that we feel we are on one side of Borges' wall, peering over at the dotty happenings on the nameless orb. The reader must be able to both be seduced as a reader and awaken for himself as a reader. The contrast must not be too harsh. The distance from the greatest intensity of dream to the most acute sense of reality must not be too great.

One way in which writers have met this challenge is by making the real world of the book seem, from the very beginning, faintly dream-like. This has the effect of making the reader feel that they are already in a dream-like ether, so when they come to a dream scene it does not seem very different from reality. Shortening the distance between dreaming and living does not necessarily destroy the other-planet feeling of dreams; it makes one feel suddenly, strikingly, near something of which one's understanding is murky and incomplete. This feeling pervades Per Petterson's novel *Out Stealing Horses* (2005), capturing as it does the morning time in cold Scandinavian winters. Grogginess, the chill off a window in the morning, nature acting erratically and of its own accord; above all, a feeling of being pulled into a meaningful world—a world that apparently wants what we have—without knowing why.

We have ourselves now, at least in theory, a recipe for writing dreams well: cushion the reader's fall into dream by investing life with some of the ambience of dreams; have the dreamer both perceive dreams and think them; make the dream world seem both near at hand and profoundly impenetrable, almost imponderable, such that its relevance to anything outside of it is a matter for discussion and further probing; allow the reader to fall into the dream world, but grant them enough of a tether to think about the dream, so that the reader can think critically and thereby awaken; allow the "I" to recede without vanishing entirely, or dilate so that it can contain many subjects.

In his novel *Waiting for the Barbarians* (1980), which tells of a magistrate living at the edge of a vast empire and his relationship with a young barbarian girl, J.M. Coetzee manages to come as close as any writer I know to writing a dream that feels authentically like a dream. Troubled by fears that the barbarian tribes that surround his remote outpost are encroaching, the Magistrate has the following dream:

> From horizon to horizon the earth is white with snow. It falls from a sky in which the source of light is diffuse and everywhere present, as though the sun has dissolved into mist, become an aura. In the dream I pass through the barracks gate, pass the bare flagpole. The square extends before me, blending at its edges into the luminous sky. Walls, trees, houses have dwindled, lost their solidity, retired over the rim of the world.

As I glide across the square, dark figures separate out from the whiteness, children at play building a snowcastle on top of which they have planted a little red flag. They are mittened, booted, muffled against the cold. Handful after handful of snow they bring, plastering the walls of their castle, filling it out. Their breath departs from them in white puffs. The rampart around the castle is half built. I strain to pierce the queer floating gabble of their voices but can make out nothing.

I am aware of my bulk, my shadowiness, therefore I am not surprised that the children melt away on either side as I approach. All but one. Older than the others, perhaps not even a child, she sits in the snow with her hooded back to me working at the door of the castle, her legs splayed, burrowing, patting, moulding. I stand behind her and watch. She does not turn. I try to imagine the face between the petals of her peaked hood but cannot.

p. 10

Coetzee does not at first indicate to the reader that he is reading a dream; rather, Coetzee creates the feeling of a dream, into which the reader wades before discovering that it is a dream. "Horizon to horizon" encloses the world, whereupon snow begins to fill it, falling and falling, the flakes fluttering downward like fish food sinking into an aquarium. It only appears that the sun illuminates this world; in fact, the illumination comes from every point in the sky. It is otherworldly, this world. "In the dream I pass through the barracks gate, pass the bare flagpole." The "I" (he, the Magistrate) now enters the dream and passes by things he knows: the description is of "the barracks gate," not "a barracks gate," "the bare flagpole," not "a bare flagpole." He is not seeing these things. He knows them. The visible world—walls, trees, houses—recedes. It does not disappear, but retires into the medium of the dream. The perceived aspects of the dream become incorporated into dream material, suggesting that the next stage of the dream will reflect aspects of all that receded. The fragmentation does not startle us; we can hold on to the expectation that the pieces will come together again, albeit in another form. The softness of the snow, the diffuseness of the light, the silence, all are decidedly soporific. The reader is not asleep, but falling asleep, while the tide of the dream draws back into the ocean of the dream-medium, creating a critical expectation in the reader of an imminent return of the tide, carrying in it new debris.

At every turn the "I," through which the reader lives the dream, is both reading the dream and being made to feel that everything in the dream is the object of a greater force. "As I glide across the square, dark figures separate out from the whiteness, children at play building a snowcastle on top of which they have planted a little red flag. They are mittened, booted, muffled against the cold." The children are "mittened" and "booted," but by whom, by what? They have, after all, "separated out" from the dream, and so are still just little pieces of the whiteness of this nameless orb. Except for a red flag: its redness reads instantly as crimson, as blood, alerting the reader to something erotic, something allied with death, whose meaning could plausibly be traced back to consciousness and the physical world.

But like the dream itself, the snowcastle is still only half built. The critical aspect of mind is self-aware enough to strain to hear and understand, but cannot "pierce" the skin of the dream.

This outright rejection of the Magistrate's attempt to listen creates an anxiety that begins to shake the Magistrate from the dream. "I am aware of my bulk, my shadowiness, therefore I am not surprised that the children melt away on either side as I approach." The "I" becomes more aware of itself, more dominant, causing the dream to seize up. The children "melt away" as the dream no longer surprises the "I." The hold that the dream has on the "I" dissipates. The physical approach of the "I" is really an emotional approach of the "I" to a distillation of the dream so significant, so intense, that the dream cannot possibly survive it. "Older than the others, perhaps not even a child, she sits in the snow with her hooded back to me working at the door of the castle, her legs splayed, burrowing, patting, moulding." The dynamics of the dream have reversed. Before, children populated the dream; they were "mittened, booted, muffled against the cold." Young and vulnerable, they need protection, though the protection given to them is precarious, as the adults who have "mittened" and "booted" them are nowhere to be found. Now, the child is on the verge of adulthood. "Mittened, booted, muffled" becomes "burrowing, patting, moulding." Instead of children steeling themselves against a cold so bitter it cannot be resisted entirely, an adult woman now constructs the barrier of a castle, insulating those who live inside.

The dream concludes, "I stand behind her and watch. She does not turn. I try to imagine the face between the petals of her peaked hood but cannot." The "I" has become dominant, almost desperate. It knows it is in a dream and wants to turn the dream into something that can be understood. First, it asserts itself by standing "behind her," making her feel the difference between the physical reality of the dreamer and the incorporeality of the object of the dream. She does not turn around or draw back. The "I" then watches, tries to turn the dream into something that can be perceived in the way life can be perceived. But "she does not turn," suggesting that the dream cannot be perceived in the way the critical faculty would like. The "I" then tries "to imagine," resorting to the conceptual, perhaps even to the bank of knowledge and memories that could be, like Nabokov's Green Fritillary, an indication that the dream is not apart from the dreamer, but an extension of the dreamer. But the imagination also fails—"I" cannot imagine the girl. The dream does not respond. Its central mystery cannot be felt or seen or imagined. If "I" cannot watch and if "I" cannot imagine, "I" can go no further. The dream comes to an end. Without seduction, without critical rewards, without observation, without concepts, the dream is over.

★★★

When I was sixteen or seventeen years old, my friend Harrison Leong had dinner with my father, mother, and I at our home in San Francisco. I do not remember how the conversation headed in such a direction, but at some point Harrison, who knew that my father was a psychoanalyst, asked him, "What is a dream?" As I remember it, my father never gave an answer; I believe the conversation went someplace else before he had a chance to respond. However, no more than a day or two later, I vividly remember my father telling me that the question that Harrison had asked him was the most interesting question any of my friends had ever asked him. I think this was a kind way of saying that this was the only interesting question my friends had ever asked him.

The question has stayed with me for twenty years. What is a dream? I have only a partial answer, which this essay has explored: a dream is what cannot be written—written well, written convincingly, written so that it is true in the way other writing is true. Yes, Coetzee comes close to capturing in words what dreaming is like, but he has succeeded in bringing to life just a fingernail of the great body of human dreams, like one who has managed to recover a single rusty spoon from an armada of sunken ships. And, to judge him objectively, it is a bent spoon, not quite what it once was. That a dream would be such a thing speaks, I think, to the fact that mystery (that which resists becoming an object of knowledge) must be present in both life and literature in order for them not to succumb to the critical faculty and therefore perish from reification. If this is true, then dreams are an inexhaustible wellspring of mystery that sustain life; and, in much the same way, draw the limit to what language can represent of life. That limit, which separates what can be said from what cannot be said, safeguards the inexpressible beyond that limit—guaranteeing the continued existence of the nameless orb and thus the continued existence of the feeling of *it makes no difference* on which a part of the mystery of dreams rests. This safeguarding of the dream world is intrinsic to the way in which we are, as Borges suggests, robbed of our dreams forever every single morning when we awake. We are powerless to hold on to dreams and powerless to preserve them as we first experienced them.

A different way of putting this is that the most important piece of writing is that which cannot be written, for it guarantees the mystery that literature requires in order to continue to hold any interest. Lawrence Raab imagines such a thing in "The Poem That Can't Be Written" (2009):

> is different from the poem
> that is not written, or the many
>
> that are never finished—those boats
> lost in the fog, adrift
>
> in the windless latitudes,
> the charts useless, the water gone.
>
> In the poem that cannot
> be written there is no danger,
>
> No ponderous cargo of meaning,
> no meaning at all. And this
>
> is its splendor, this is how
> it becomes an emblem,

> not of failure or loss,
> but of the impossible.
>
> So the wind rises. The tattered sails
> billow, and the air grows sweeter.
>
> A green island appears.
> Everyone is saved.

A dream is a poem that cannot be written. It is an emblem, as Raab says, of the impossible. Like Borges' "nameless orb," it is a ship without cargo, on its way to nowhere. But we, as the writers and dreamers, in writing a dream, provide the cargo, coax the boat to where we would like it to dock, drawing in an island, and thereby saving ourselves. We can't draw the boat, only the island.

PART IV
Brief interlude

8

INSIDE THE MAGIC CIRCLE

On Homero Aridjis' *The Child Poet*

I had intended to write at greater length about Mexican poet Homero Aridjis' strange, beautiful memoir *The Child Poet* ([1971]2016). However, the introduction to the book, written by Aridjis' daughter, who has translated *The Child Poet* from Spanish into English, is itself a piece of literature so fine that I cannot seem to get beyond it to comment on the father's work. The English introduction to *El poeta niño* is so essential to what the father was trying to say when he first wrote down his recollections of his early life that it has brought to completion an autobiography that would be unfinished without it. Chloe Aridjis has not only translated and introduced her father's memories of his boyhood; she has supplied what was missing from them, almost as if she had defied time and biology and played a part in the life he led before she was born.

Homero Aridjis must have always intended—consciously or unconsciously—that his daughter play the part she has in this work. Perhaps it is common for the poet-parent to have fantasies of a newborn translator, not a co-author but an *after-author*, to write out dimensions of his own life that he either cannot see or cannot describe. "My father has always said that he was born twice," begins the introduction.

> The first time was to his mother, Josefina, in April 1940, and the second time was as a poet, in January 1951. His life was distinctively cleaved in two. Before that fateful Saturday he was carefree and confident, the youngest of five brothers growing up in the small Mexican village of Contepec, Michoacán. After the accident—in which he nearly died on the operating table after shooting himself with a shotgun his brothers had left propped against the bedroom wall—he became a shy, introspective child who spent afternoons reading Homer and writing poems and stories at the dining room table instead of playing soccer with his schoolmates.

p. 7

In these sentences we see the daughter's nearly invisible hand. Her father is both her subject and a parent whom she cares for in the process of presenting him to the reader: she supplies a fact that belongs to the objective world ("Josefina, in April 1940"), and then matches it with a poetic touch by having the J in January play off of the J in Josefina. This makes the first month of the year, January, into a mother to the poet, existing side by side with Josefina, the mother to the infant. (This doubling of the J is an effect of the translation into English, as January in Spanish begins with an e, *enero*, and so would not pair with Josefina in the original). The daughter does not have her young father, Homero, read just any author; she has him reading his namesake, Homer. In this way, the child-poet Homero is born into not just a Mexican family but also a poetic lineage. He has biological parents as well as poetic parents, the latter being Janus (the God of beginnings and transitions, namesake of January) and Homer. Just as Homero created Mrs. Aridjis biologically, Mrs. Aridjis creates Homero poetically by making him the progeny of Homer. All this is done lightly, so that it reads not as an editing but as a curation of a life. In taking such care, Mrs. Aridjis is not just being a good prefacer; she is also being a good daughter. The intimacy is carried in the relationship the daughter has to her father as a poet and in the loving relationship she has to her father's style in her translation.

Everything that happened before the accident with the shotgun, we learn, remained a secret to the poet himself until he was over forty years old.

> After the accident his early childhood became like a locked garden. And then, in 1971, the memories found a way out. As soon as my mother became pregnant with me, visions from this elusive period started returning to my father in astonishingly vivid dreams, giving shape to what would become *El poeta niño*, a celebration of his life before 1951. Imminent fatherhood helped revive memories that had, for two decades, lain dormant.
>
> *p.* 7

The phrase "found a way out" captures the energy of children, and memories, to emerge. It not only draws an analogy between an unborn child and a vividly unremembered memory but also juxtaposes the fixed gestation of natural birth to the sometimes interminable gestation of certain memories. Tellingly, at the moment when Homero finds his way back into his "locked" past, the aesthetic future of these memories—the one who will translate them, introduce them to the world, care for them, understand them better than anyone else—is born. This recalls how Homero is linked, by birth, to Janus (via January), as Janus is usually depicted as having two faces, one looking forward into the future and the other backward into the past. In other words, as Homero originally wrote it, the coming into being of the daughter brings into being the person who can, at last, remember the past, and so begin the writing of the book. Biology (the birth of the daughter who rouses the past) and aesthetics (the birth of the daughter who will finish the process of writing down the past that has been roused) meet in the figure of

Mrs. Aridjis. She is the father-poet's fantasy of a daughter-translator come to life. That she grew to fulfill this fantasy seems almost too perfect to be true.

We see here that the care for the biological person and the care of their language are two sides of the same coin. Chloe Aridjis cares for her father *in language*; she does not advise him as a person—she revises his style. This ability to care for a person in language—and to care for the language they use—is a dimension of poetic creation and refinement rarely so clearly visible as in this book. It is also, so Homero Aridjis' depiction of the first few years of his life illustrates, a kind of care that has its origins in the first years of life. Here is how Homero describes the sense of security under which the body and the language of poetry can develop:

> I was surrounded by a magic circle, which no one should enter. This circle protected my intimacy, with its baggage of thoughts, fears, and desires. What I felt mattered only to me. To reveal my thoughts would mean revealing myself, to exhibit my desires meant exhibiting myself. And if I asked for something and it was denied me, my entire self felt rejected, for I had disclosed one of my soul's necessities and placed it at someone else's mercy. For this reason I did things on my own. And if someone went off because I didn't show my interest, I would let that person go: their being remained within my being, in my thoughts.
>
> *p. 20*

He goes on to describe how, physically and emotionally, he came to be the kind of boy who could be a home to his own words even when the outside world was indifferent to the profoundly alive language coming into being within him:

> And if, when with friends, I grew excited by the sight of some sunflowers or an ash tree, or if I discovered the shadow of a cloud cast onto the mountain, or if, gazing at a chestnut tress, I saw a drop of water on a slanted leaf sliding from center to edge, slowly descending as if on a slope, I would realize, thanks to the near deafness with which they listened to me, that I was moved by things that did not interest them, and that my words to them made a pointless journey, as pointless as an elevator in which someone has pressed all the buttons so that it stops at every floor and opens its doors without ever getting on or off.
>
> *p. 21*

I would venture that, though Homero Aridjis had become a widely published poet by the time he wrote this, he still felt that these memories—which are built of words—could not survive being plunged into the cold waters of the external world. The language in which these memories had been encoded still lived within the "magic circle" and as such could not be revealed without his suffering the feeling of having "my entire self rejected" because he had put the language of the self "at someone else's mercy." Only with the imminent birth of someone who could draw a magic circle around the larger world and so contain the art that the memories desired to become could Homero retrieve the words necessary to describe his formative years. The magic circle drawn by Chloe Aridjis is as integral to the artistic success of *The Child Poet* as the smaller magic circle it holds inside of it.

PART V

Neither out far nor in deep

9

THE PREDICAMENT OF PSYCHOANALYSIS AND LITERATURE[1]

This chapter is written in response to several feelings I have had about the field of psychoanalytic literary criticism, feelings that have developed in the course of closely studying, and contributing to, the field over several years. My feelings concern three matters: how the field of psychoanalytic literary criticism defines itself, and the reason that it defines itself in the way that it does; the specific way in which psychoanalytic ideas and terms are brought to bear on literature by psychoanalytic critics; and how criticism and literature are understood to relate to one another by those working in the field of psychoanalytic criticism. Which is to say, my thinking concerns the field itself, its reading practices, and the nature of its cross-disciplinarity.

I use the word "feelings" to describe these lines of thinking because I know very well that my conception of psychoanalytic literary criticism is not an objective assessment of how the field really is, but only my personal experience of the field currently. In what follows I draw upon the challenges and concerns that arise whenever I start the process of working within the field as a literary critic and scholar. In the first section of the paper I address the rationale that underlies how the field of psychoanalytic literary criticism has come to define itself, and the con-sequences of this rationale for the critic who would like to bring to bear on literature aspects and dimensions of psychoanalysis that lie outside of this definition. In the second section I discuss the preconceptions about literature that seem to lie behind how psychoanalysis frequently reads literature and demonstrate how these pre-conceptions run counter to the inner-workings of literature as I understand them. The final section of the paper considers first how the relationship of psychoanalysis to literature is too often one in which psychoanalysis is used to explain or "solve" literature and then how one can reimagine the relationship of each field to the other in a way that brings the fields parallel to one another without demanding that either of them be applied demonstratively to the other. In the latter two sec-tions, I introduce terms and technologies from the visual arts (specifically, anamorphic art and the stereoscope) to offer as clear an illustration as I can of how literary language coheres to create an artistic effect and how criticism and literature could be conceived anew in relation to one another.

In every case, my thinking reflects my position as a literary scholar; as such, this paper is marked by a heightened awareness of what happens to literature when psychoanalysis is brought to bear on it, and by an explicit attention to preserving what is most vital and irreducible about literature, against any lingering tendency of psychoanalytic criticism to restrain literature within an interpretation or formulation that reduces it to anything less than it is.

Though this chapter is meant to be of use to those who work in the field of psychoanalytic literary criticism, it is more widely intended for anyone who believes that the process by which two fields are brought together is a precarious one; that often one field is made the hero at the expense of the other, or what each field most has to offer the other is left unexpressed or unprovided, or—and this is my feeling of psychoanalysis and literature—that neither field has quite been able to tell the other exactly how it works or what it is, so that neither field has wholly yielded its secret to the other. A great deal of interesting and valuable work has come about due to interdisciplinary thinking that spans psychoanalysis and literature, but alongside this work there continues to be a prevailing feeling that, when psychoanalysis is brought to bear on literature, some essential aspect of literature is lost; and, in the same way, that something essential about psychoanalytic thinking may not be adequately represented in psychoanalytic literary criticism. Psychoanalysis and literature may be, I am saying, like the narrator of Lucia Berlin's story "A Manual for Cleaning Women," who remarks: "Some lady at a bridge party some-where started the rumor that to test the honesty of a cleaning woman you leave little rosebud ashtrays around with loose change in them, here and there" (p. 27). To this, the cleaning woman says: "My solution to this is to always add a few pennies, even a dime" (p. 27). It sometimes feels to me that this is the state of psychoanalytic literary criticism: the passing back and forth the loose change of our fields, under the suspicion that one or both parties are being shorted in the exchange.

This paper attempts to clarify exactly why it is that a psychoanalytic approach to literature often seems, to those working from within literature, to overlook or fail to appreciate what is inimitable and irreplaceable about literature (to, in effect, take out of literature what makes it literature in the first place). It likewise clarifies how the underlying rationale defining psychoanalytic literary criticism makes it difficult to express, within the confines of the field, certain essential aspects of psycho-analysis. Further, the paper describes a model for understanding the vital aspect of literature that frequently seems to get lost in analytic interpretation, and from this to propose a binocular model for bringing psychoanalysis and literature together.

How the field of psychoanalytic literary criticism defines itself

Those who write about the relationship of psychoanalysis to literature are all effectively faced with the same task: to locate the psychoanalytic in the literature without reducing the literature to psychoanalysis. The process by which this feat is accomplished, or isn't accomplished, is the process of writing psychoanalytic literary criticism. This process can, of course, take many different forms and lead to any number of results. Psychoanalysis has, in important respects, moved beyond the psychobiographical and pathological readings of art and literature proposed by Freud. It was able to do this once it became conscious that such a method turned literature into a demonstration of psychoanalytic theory. Out of this realization came a host of theories concerning the creative impulse and the psychological origins of art (Milner 1950; Segal 1952, 1991; Ehrenzweig 1971; Winnicott 1971; Meltzer and Harris-Williams 1988); the role of form and style in creating artistic effect or ideological force (Stokes 1965, Schafer 1994; Jacobus 2005; Moss 2012; Mahon 2013); the many shades of awareness and listening held in common by the reader of literature and the psychoanalyst (Akhtar 2013; Griffin 2016); and several works of fiction and semi-autobiography by psychoanalysts (Fuller 1981; Bion 1991). Though orthodox applications of psychoanalysis have not died out, one can detect in the field of psychoanalytic literary criticism an awareness of the problem I am pointing to and the beginning of several significant attempts to correct it or redirect the field away from it.

Nonetheless, underlying the field of psychoanalytic literary criticism is, I find, a fairly consistent logic, one that must be confronted and addressed if the field of psychoanalytic literary criticism is to understand the rationale that defines its relationship to literature. This logic, I maintain, motivates even those works of analytic criticism that have attempted to move away from the more psychologically programmatic, allegorical readings of literature that were *de rigueur* between sixty and ninety years ago. In what follows, I describe the logic that underpins psychoanalytic literary criticism, and explain why it is in many ways responsible for what I perceive to be some problems and limitations that beset the field.

It is widely believed that for literary criticism to be identified as psychoanalytic it must possess, or put to use, some aspect of the psychoanalytic essence, which in this context I take to mean that which is unique to psychoanalysis in contradistinction to other fields of study and other forms of criticism. If something does not contain any literary essence it is not literary; likewise, if something does not contain any psychoanalytic essence it is not psychoanalytic. Therefore, if we wish to prove that literature is psychoanalytic, or that an interpretation of literature merits being called psychoanalytic, at minimum it must contain or reflect or invoke some part of the psychoanalytic essence. Otherwise, there is no support for attaching the adjective "psychoanalytic" to the noun "literature."

Problematically, the way in which critics have gone about demonstrating that their reading carries in it a psychoanalytic essence, or that the work of literature that they are addressing expresses something distinctly analytic, is by making use of psychoanalytic elements or finding in the literature psychoanalytic properties. When I speak of elements, I refer to terminology, concepts, logics, or methodologies that are immediately associated with or derived from psychoanalytic theory or practice. Elements are most often used in one of two ways: an element is introduced by the critic to explain some facet of the text, or it is understood by the critic to be embodied in the text. In the former case, literature is decoded by, or represented in the terms of, psychoanalysis; as when Edmund Wilson (1976) "rewrites" Henry James's ghost story *The Turn of the Screw* (1991) as a tale of neurotic sexual repression, thereby using an analytic element to "solve" the riddle of an otherwise ambiguous story. In the latter case, the text may live out, in character or author or configuration, a psychological structure or dynamic, lending credence to the existence and function of a structure or dynamic that is central to psychoanalytic thinking. Peter Brooks, for instance, argues that plot itself, in being inherently programmed to move toward closure, enacts or lives out the death-drive. In either case, the reason that the criticism is deemed psychoanalytic is because of the presence and use of elements; without these elements the works by Wilson and Brooks would not be considered psychoanalytic works of criticism.

The problem with such a rationale is that two things that are not equivalent have been conflated: psychoanalytic elements stand in as representative of the psychoanalytic essence (by "essence" I mean that which makes a work tax-onomically appropriate for a psychoanalytic publication or for the designation "psychoanalytic," not the true or natural substance of the entire field). Psycho-analytic elements, in this scenario, are what make a reading psychoanalytic—their presence "moves" the criticism out of the broad field of criticism and into the specific field of psychoanalytic criticism, the way red and green ornaments turn a pine tree into a Christmas tree. If analytic terms—such as "transference," "reaction formation," "pleasure principle," "drive theory," "depressive position"—appear often enough, the criticism is allowed a place in the field of psychoanalytic literary criticism. And because, as I demonstrated earlier, something becomes psychoanalytic when it possesses something of the psychoanalytic essence, elements are that which grant a work of criticism the psychoanalytic essence it needs for it to be deemed psychoanalytic. Elements, one might say, are the price of admission for inclusion in the field of psychoanalytic literary criticism. As such, from the perspective of literary studies, elements are the only way that psychoanalysis announces that it is there, and so we assume that psychoanalysis is nothing more than its elements. Elements become metonymic for psychoanalysis as a whole.

A quite significant portion of psychoanalytic literary criticism, I am saying, takes the basis of its own psychoanalytic nature to lie in its use, or discovery, of elements. This is the case with psychobiological readings of authors and characters (Bonaparte 1949; Jones 1949; Greenacre 1955; Crews 1966; Bergman 2013); with the sub-limation and censorship of the creative process (Freud 1908; Kris 1952; Irwin 1980; Bloom 1982); with literary texts decoded by, or presented as illustrative of, a vari-ety of psychoanalytic concepts and dynamics (Felman 1982; Berman 1990; Kogan 2014; Manolopoulos 2015; Houlding 2015; Aalen 2017); with the structure and design of plot and narrative (Johnson [1977]1982; Brooks 1994); with the psycholo-gical responses evoked in readers (Holland 1968; Rose 1980; Priel 2011). Presented with any of the abovementioned works of psychoanalytic criticism, one can ask: what makes this reading, or this work, psychoanalytic? Why does it have "psychoanalysis" in its title? Why does it appear in a psychoanalytic journal; been published by an analytic press; come to be anthologized beside Freud or Jung or Klein? The answer, almost invariably, is the presence of psychoanalytic elements—it follows the logic by which elements are made equivalent to the essence of psychoanalysis.

Consequently, the psychoanalytic literary critic is compelled to bring to bear his psychoanalytic thinking *in the form of elements*. The assumptions of the field all but require element-based criticism. Two outcomes follow from this, both of which have enormous consequences for the field of psychoanalytic literary criticism and the thinking of the analytic critic. First, the psychoanalytic critic is practically provoked to address literature with psychoanalytic elements and formulations, even though he may feel strongly that what is most important to the literature cannot be contained in elements and formulations. The critic is put in the position of having to address literature with concepts and tools that, he may feel, are extrinsic to it. The predicament is that the critic must behave as if literature cannot be psychoanalytic until it is shown to have some of the properties of psychoanalysis; but he also agrees that none of these properties and terms are in fact necessary to the literature, for the literature contains everything that we mean to express in these terms without the use of them. And yet, if he does not call attention to psychoanalytic elements he, under the current arrangement, cannot place his work under the banner of psychoanalytic literary criticism. The psychoanalytic literary critic is trapped by the parameters of the field: he is reluctant to impose upon literature elements and concepts that he knows to be extrinsic to it, but if he does not impose such elements he cannot work as a psychoanalytic critic.

Second, if the psychoanalytic literary critic feels compelled to present psychoanalytic thinking in the form of elements, it becomes exceedingly difficult to present psychoanalysis in any other way but in elements. If elements are effectively no different from psychoanalysis itself, the meaning of psychoanalysis within the field is restricted solely to what is communicated about psychoanalysis in its elements. No room is left for what psychoanalysis can mean absent its elements. Without elements, criticism no longer has a psychoanalytic calling card, and is thereby excluded from the field of psychoanalytic literary criticism (at least as it is currently defined). Elements are the gatekeeper, leaving those who bring to bear their understanding of psychoanalysis in their criticism in forms other than by elements out in the cold.

I am suggesting that a great deal of criticism that is psychoanalytic, and deserves that appellation, may never be regarded as such, which impoverishes the vitality of the field and leaves out dimensions of psychoanalysis that would be of the most value to one wishing to deepen their understanding of literature. Psychoanalytic literary criticism should not confine itself to an element-based definition of psychoanalysis. Of course, several questions arise here: what do you mean by literary criticism that is psychoanalytic without elements? Isn't the essence of psychoanalysis comprised of its elements? How else but through its prototypical features could psychoanalysis cordon off a specific subset of literary criticism for itself?

As a response to these questions, I will here introduce a work of literary criticism that expresses something vital about psychoanalysis without breathing a word about its properties: Randall Jarrell's essay "To the Laodiceans" (1999), in which Jarrell discusses Robert Frost's poem, "Neither Out Far Nor in Deep."

I wish to be clear that in trying to describe how Jarrell's essay manages to be psychoanalytic without the use of psychoanalytic elements I am not proposing a metric by which any work of criticism can be deemed psychoanalytic or non-psychoanalytic. Rather, I am proposing that there exists a kind of criticism that is psychoanalytic, but neither by virtue of the elements that it employs nor by virtue of its general connection to, or position within, a Western culture that is permeated by psychoanalysis (by this latter measure, all criticism could be called psycho-analytic). In such a psychoanalytic-literary space, psychoanalysis is neither refined into elements nor dissolved into a vague cultural indebtedness. I am concerned with the work that can be done between these two extremes.[2] This paper does not claim to define the parameters of this middle-space; nor does it aim to define a list of features that a work of criticism must exemplify in order to qualify for inclusion in this space. Such a task would be doomed from the outset: there is no finite list of attributes that define psychoanalysis, and what will be psychoanalytic about a work cannot be defined beforehand (much as the specific psychoanalytic work with a patient cannot be defined beforehand). Furthermore, the nature of the space cannot be known beforehand: it is a product of the desire one has to express the intuition that the space is there, and of one's attempt to create and work within the space in the act of writing. Ultimately, this paper is presenting the very beginning of an unending process of probing, and creating, the boundaries of the space; it does this while simultaneously attempting to describe precisely and vividly what appears to me to be unmistakably analytic about Jarrell's work.

Here is the Frost poem to which Jarrell responds in his essay:

> The people along the road
> All turn and look one way
> They turn their back on the land
> They look at the sea all day.
>
> As long as it takes to pass
> A ship keeps raising its hull;
> The wetter ground like glass
> Reflects a standing gull.
>
> The land may vary more;
> But wherever the truth may be —
> The water comes ashore,
> And the people look at the sea.
>
> They cannot look out far,
> They cannot look in deep.

> But when was that ever a bar
> To any watch they keep?
> > *Frost, 1969, p. 301*

In his response, Jarrell first compares Frost's poem to a poem by A.E. Housman, and then writes:

> But Frost's poem is flatter, grayer, and at once tenderer and more terrible, without even the consolations of rhetoric and exaggeration—there is no "primal fault"[3] in Frost's poem, but only the faint Biblical memories of "any watch they keep." What we do know we don't care about; what we do care about we don't know: we can't look out very far, or in very deep; and when did that ever bother *us*? It would be hard to find anything more unpleasant to say about people than that last stanza: but Frost doesn't say it unpleasantly—he says it with flat ease, takes everything with something harder than contempt, more passive than acceptance. And isn't there something heroic about the whole business, too—something touching about our absurdity? If the fool persisted in his folly he would become a wise man, Blake said, and we have persisted. The tone of the last lines—or, rather, their careful suspension between several tones, as a piece of iron can be held in the air between powerful enough magnets—allows for this too. This recognition of the essential limitations of man, without denial or protest or rhetoric or palliation, is very rare and very valuable, and rather usual in Frost's best poetry.
>
> > *p. 21*

This passage from Jarrell is not psychoanalytic literary criticism; it is literary criticism that is personal to psychoanalysis; it gives us the best of psychoanalysis, its characteristics as identifiable as any element to one who has a mind of psychoanalysis. It does not apply psychoanalysis; it speaks for its permanent concerns, and seems to know how to write in a voice in which psychoanalysis is very true, just as the poet knows how to write in a voice in which poetry is very true.

If I do not become more specific this will all sound, to borrow a phrase from William Gass, very "country headed" (1979, p. 27). So what is it, exactly, that is psychoanalytic about Jarrell's reading? To answer this, one must make psychoanalysis into a word of one's own, not a word of any history or institution. As Dostoevsky said, "Why do we have a mind, if not to get our own way?" (Qtd. in Koolhaas 1977, p. 320). To conclude this section of the paper, I will discuss three ways in which Jarrell's reading of Frost speaks forcefully for psychoanalysis.

1 *What we do know we don't care about; what we do care about we don't know: we can't look out very far, or in very deep; and when did that ever bother* us?

In this sentence, it does not matter whether any phrase—or really any truth—is formulated as a question or as an assertion. This is the ethic of the sentence: a question must be at least as true, if not truer, than its answer. The knowable and the unknowable (bare philosophical categories) are transformed into what Jarrell later calls the "humanly understable or [the] humanly unununderstandable" (p. 32). It may not be clear if the assertions that feel so true in the moment of reading them are as true as they seem (do we really not care about what we know?), but this is our illusion, our task; we are in a place where we are still deciding if what is said is a question or an answer. *And when did that ever bother us?* There is such decency and tenderness to this question, such love and camaraderie. It puts its arm around the rest of that sad, straining sentence and gives a squeeze. What question could ever be a better defense against the defenselessness of the "humanly unununderstandable"? What question could better express the charming, denial-ridden bullheadedness that one needs to continue looking when one cannot look out very far or in very deep?

2 *It would be hard to find anything more unpleasant to say about people than that last stanza: but Frost doesn't say it unpleasantly—he says it with flat ease, takes everything with something harder than contempt, more passive than acceptance.*

Jarrell notices that at certain moments the affronts that Frost throws at humans are so indicting of their essential nature that it would be too cruel of him to write such true observations. So instead he says them. There are things he says and things he doesn't say, but Frost is not about to hide himself in rhetoric. Jarrell makes us feel the choice Frost faces, with what conscience he must have deliberated over how to present an unpleasant truth, and the language he decided would be best for getting the reader to level with themselves about the role they play in unpleasant matters. The poem puts Frost in the position of having to ask himself: how do I say this? How hard do I need to be, and how soft? The immediacy of the philosophy of Frost's poem is heartbreaking. *And when did that ever bother us?* Now it bothers us, deeply; and Frost knows that what he has to say will bother us, because it so clearly bothers him. Frost must make us as defenseless as he possibly can without running us out of the poem—out of life, out of psychoanalytic self-reflection—entirely.

3 *The tone of the last lines—or, rather, their careful suspension between several tones, as a piece of iron can be held in the air between powerful enough magnets—allows for this too.*

A lot of what passes for tone, Jarrell informs us, is in fact more accurately language onto which several tones are being pressed, so that the language becomes for the moment a pure feat of tone. At such moments, the tone breaks in upon the sense of the poem with such astounding intensity that the absurdity of trying to compress so much emotion and "truth-directed" (Coetzee 1992, p. 261) thinking into so few words crashes down on the reader, causing us to say, along with Frost, that "It took that pause to make him realize the mountain he was climbing" (Frost 1942, "Time Out," p. 323). As Jarrell implies, nearly says outright, we must believe in the heroism of absurd ventures in order not to be dispirited by the more daunting aspects of absurdity. Tone is the proper place for this heroism because the heroism is an aspect of the humble lyric mood of the poem and the critique, not an abstract idea that has a natural place in the structure of ideas on which the poem is built. Tone is more than an inflection here. It is 'the obstinately gentle air" (Frost 1969, "Time Out," p. 323) that "allows for" emotions and convictions that would be merely absurd anywhere else.

Jarrell writes so well that there is no need of elements at all; where would you even put one? But nothing has been left out. Jarrell inspires us to consider, and take to heart, enormously important questions. He grounds such questions in interpenetrated tones; in truths against which we are psychologically defenseless; in the responsibilities and fears that come with having to speak with "flat ease" words that may pierce just a foot or two away; and he has done these many things not for himself but for Frost. What's more, even if one did wish to make elements out of Jarrell's essay, what elements could be made from it? Tone, in a pinch, could be treated as an element. But Jarrell has so redefined tone for his own purposes that it no longer has any legitimate connection to the element "tone" as it would be invoked by, say, your average English professor. Tone, in Jarrell's hands, is not a staid concept that can be applied anywhere because Jarrell has made something *of* tone. In every respect, this is psychoanalytic criticism, and Jarrell should have an analytic field that welcomes him.

Reading with elements: what elements cannot say about literature

Having dealt with the effect of analytic elements on the field and on the critic's freedom, I will now turn to the use of analytic elements as a reading practice in its own right. I will assess applied psychoanalysis as a form of literary interpretation.

As I said earlier, it is my feeling that to apply psychoanalytic elements to literature is to fail to understand something about how literature works, something that is of the very essence of literature. To be even stronger in my language, the application of elements to literature represents a fatal misunderstanding of how literature takes on meaning. I do not believe I am alone in this feeling, as it is not uncommon to hear that psychoanalysis ought not to be transposed onto literature. But in my experience so far, rarely do we get a sustained explanation for why exactly such readings are undesirable. My question is: why are such readings objectionable, and what can we learn from such readings about the nature of literature and the task of the critic?

In addressing this question, it is important to note that the application of elements is not of necessity a bad thing. In other circumstances, the application of discrete elements may meet the requirements of a worthwhile interpretation. However, in our specific case, in which the object of study is literature, it seems to me that so long as psychoanalysis bases itself upon elements it will always violate an important, and in this case burning, principal, which is that art, like psychoanalysis, is unpredictable; what matters most in it cannot be explained ahead of time. And because it is unpredictable, it must be treated as such. It is the violation of this predictability that, in the broadest sense, explains why analytic criticism is sometimes thought to mistreat, or misrepresent, literature. Face to face with literature, psychoanalysis leans upon pre-existent elements, and what it suffers most from is the accusation that its elements make of literature something already predicted by psychoanalysis. Literature, subjected to this maneuver by psychoanalysis, becomes an example of psychoanalytic art, rather than what it is, an event in its own life. "Talk, laugh, move," the painter Manet would tell his models: "to look real you must be alive" (Barnes 2015, p. 110). The essence of literature—its reality—is its unpredictability, and in rendering it predictable we steal its life. The same is true of psychoanalysis itself (including psychoanalytic writing and criticism): it is unpredictable at its best, and any effort to reduce analysis to elements is an attempt to render it predictable and therefore lifeless.

It is, then, literature's responsibility to be unpredictable and the critic's responsibility to allow it to remain so. This requires that we not anticipate literature, that we not foresee our own image in it. But in the same breath it also requires that there be something unpredictable about the interpretations we propose. The critic, too, must be unpredictable, for it is of the essence of criticism as well to be unpredictable. When one of Cézanne's models made the mistake of falling asleep, he roared: "Wretch! You've ruined the pose! I tell you in all seriousness you must hold it like an apple. Does an apple move?" (Barnes 2015, p. 110). Though art is alive, the critic is also alive, and he must not, as Cezanne understood, allow the art to predict him, to tell him what to paint and how to paint it. It is within his rights to paint an apple. And it is also within his rights to frustrate the art he examines; to do nothing with it or less with it than the art would have hoped. One model reported that Degas spent the entire four hours of her posing session combing her hair (Barnes 2015, p. 120).

The predicament of psychoanalysis and literature can, then, be traced back to the widespread practice of allowing elements to stand in for essence. The result is a criticism made of elements predicting itself in literature reduced to elements. We see now that the analytic critic who hopes to work against the powerful tide of elements-based criticism is faced with two great challenges: the first is understanding the unpredictable essence of art, its nature and its reason for being unpredictable. The second is properly treating the essence of art once it has been found and understood, and treating it in some other way than by elements.

Let us turn, then, to the first of these challenges. The unpredictable essence of literature derives, above all, from the nature of literary representation, by which I mean the relationship between literary language and the artistic essence that it expresses. I do not intend to drag out that old chestnut about how the word "tree" is an arbitrary symbol, and therefore a lackluster substitute, for the object it is meant to denote. I mean simply that the "place" where literary language makes its true point of impression—where it forms an impression that is unpredictable, but nonetheless the generative source of the artistic effect of the work—is never in a predictable relationship to the language that collectively creates this impression. The artistic essence cannot be accurately predicted from the language that has created it. There is no calculation by which either writer or critic can foretell with complete accuracy the essence of a work from even the closest examination of the language of the work or the life and times of the author.

To clarify what I mean by an unpredictable relationship between literary language and artistic essence, I am going to draw an analogy, one that I hope will give the reader a way of visualizing the mechanics of writing, language, and artistic essence as they relate to one another. The analogy is between, on the one hand, literary representation and, on the other hand, a particular kind of visual representation known as mirror anamorphosis, or anamorphic art. Mirror anamorphosis is a style of drawing in which distorted images drawn onto a piece of paper are reconstituted as a recognizable, undistorted image in the surface of a cylindrical mirror, as seen here:

FIGURE 9.1 Aaron Johnson from *Direction of the Road* by Ursula K. Le Guin; Aaron Johnson; Michael Bixler, published by Foolscap Press, © 2007.

To create an anamorphic projection, place a cylindrical mirror—like a soda can with a reflective surface—at the center of a sheet of paper, so that the surface of the paper is reflected in the mirror. Due to the curvature of the mirror, if a straight line is drawn on the paper its reflection in the mirror is distorted; the straight line on the paper is reflected in the mirror as a parabola. Therefore, to draw a straight line in the mirror, a curve must be drawn on the paper. Curved lines on the paper are reflected as straight lines in the mirror.

Drawing this way is, as the artist William Kentridge says, "counter-intuitive, not allowing the hand to make the familiar gestures and habits of a lifetime" (2016, p. 121). To make a familiar image in the mirror one must learn to draw an unfamiliar, distorted image on the paper. To draw in this way requires knowing the relationship between the initial point of impression (on the paper) and the ultimate image (the reflection in the mirror). Without an understanding of the unique causality that turns distortions into clear images, one will always end up with two distortions, one on the paper and one on the mirror. Drawing will be impossible.

With practice one can learn to predict in the distorted and unnatural markings on the paper the corrected, desired reflection in the mirror. The artist, once he or she understands the ratios and proportions that dictate the relationship between the lines on the paper and the lines in the mirror, can turn a distorted two-dimensional image in one place into a corrected three-dimensional image in another. The immediately identifiable image is skillfully predicted from what would otherwise appear to be an abstract drawing.

The unpredictability of literary language can, I believe, be grasped if one recognizes that literature functions in a way that is comparable to, but not identical with, anamorphic projection. Consider, first, the similarities between the writer and the drawer of anamorphic projection. The writer, like the artist of mirror anamorphosis, makes marks upon a page, and he too finds that the marks that he makes on the page are distorted: the collection of markings on the paper, taken at face value, make up nothing more than, at one level, strings of indecipherable glyphs, and at a deeper level, a mere recoding of external reality into a symbolic form. However, if the writer understands the inner workings of literary representation, he knows that the words and sentences he puts to paper are not symbols that approximate the reality he is attempting to describe, but distorted lines that cohere into a final artistic impression somewhere other than in language.

A case in point would be Carson McCullers' *The Heart is a Lonely Hunter* (1940), which begins simply enough, "In the town there were two mutes, and they were always together" (p. 3). The literary essence of this sentence—the source of its artistic force, the reason it succeeds as an opening—is certainly not to be found in the reality the words describe (a bare diagram of characters and their positions), but in how these distortions collectively build toward an essential impression. The sentence is written not for the sake of depiction (its two-dimensional report of character and place), but for the sake of the three-dimensional reality that these distortions are collectively forming at the point where the essence of the work could be said to reside. The cumulative effect of the language so far exceeds the words that have created the effect that the reader is left in wonderment as to how McCullers has created such literary force in such prosody. The effect is impossible to predict from the cause, which leads the reader to experience the words on the page as being in an unpredictable relationship to the force that they carry. Thought of in terms of anamorphosis, it is an opening sentence written for the cylindrical mirror, not for the flat page. To read the sentence as if it were just relaying information about two silent friends would be tantamount to looking at an anamorphic drawing without realizing that the drawing was created to be viewed via a cylindrical mirror—one would not know what the drawing was of, nor know to look elsewhere for its chief effect. This amounts to saying that the writer is an anamorphic artist, and his work must be read as such. The writer always writes with a mirror in mind, some sense that the reality he appears to describe has its most fundamental reality—takes its three-dimensional form—somewhere else. This "somewhere else," as I call it, is the essence of the work.

However, it would be facile to equate writing with anamorphosis and consider the analogy complete, for the writer works under different constraints from the visual artist; these constraints underscore the important differences between the exigencies of each art form. To start with, the visual artist can determine precisely the relationship between the initial impression on the paper and the last impression in the mirror. He can, in other words, predict with complete certainty how the movement of the pen on paper will register on the surface of the mirror. The correspondence of the distortion to the correction can be known, and once known, relied upon to hold true. It is a matter of mathematical ratios, after all. Furthermore, the artist can, if he is concerned that his proportions are inexact, check his work in the mirror; he can look right into the mirror as he draws a line, feel his hand move across the paper as the reflected line appears before his eyes. He can ensure that the essence of the drawing is following precisely from the markings that create it.

The writer, however, does not have such advantages. There is no reliable way for the writer to predict how the movement of his pen will register in the mirror whose surface reflects the essence of his work—there is no aspect ratio between the words on the paper and the essence of the literature. How can one know what final impression a given distortion—perhaps the phrase "the prudent partner of my blood" (Tennyson 1899, p. 142)—will produce in the essence of art? McCullers certainly could not inspect the essence of her opening line to be sure that it aligned perfectly with the words on the page. The image in the mirror can never be predicted, or known, with certainty from the language on the page. No surefire correspondence can be found between the words on the paper and the corrected image that they form in the mirror (the essence) of the work.

Moreover, even if the transformation from distorted language to coherent essence could be executed with complete accuracy, the writer would still be working in an unpredictable medium, for he can never in fact look into the mirror on which he writes because the mirror has neither a physical form nor a reliable psychological position from which to "look" directly at it. The best he can do is to fastidiously control the formal makeup of his work and try to gauge, through a mixture of intuition and experience, whether his distorted words are somewhere being gathered into a form that is artistically real. This is what it means to write. Without this essence-seeking intuition—this feeling of circling a focal point that remains out of view—writing is out of the question.

I like to picture the Writer, pen in hand, hunched at his desk over a circular piece of paper covered in writing, his neck chained so that he cannot look to the left or the right, with a looming, cylindrical mirror towering behind him—he cannot turn around to see what image the words he writes on the page project in the mirror. He knows that the words he writes are distortions that can only become art if they are reflected properly in the mirror behind him, but he can never turn around to examine or take the measure of the essence of what he writes. For that reason, the writer ultimately cannot know the form that the essence of his work takes, whether that form is an image, a word, an idea, a feeling, or something that is beyond envisaging. *Legible language is the cause of illegible essence.* The essence can't be expressed, but it can be reflected.

This bears on how psychoanalytic literary criticism must operate—and on any assessment of applied psychoanalysis as a reading practice. It is imperative that the critic understands his own critical work in relation to the anamorphic dynamics of literary representation. It follows from this that any critic who works simply by elements is failing to live up to this imperative, because an element is nothing more than a distortion (a line on the page that is warped unless refined in a curved mirror); it is the ready-made, pre-existent distortion of another writer. An element may best be thought of as particular squiggle on the page, one that is relied upon to cast upon the cylindrical mirror a reliable form; it is an anamorphic stencil, passed around and used by many because, many wrongly suppose, it keeps its shape wherever it is used.

But to think that elements can be used to project a reliable shape violates what we know about the relationship between the language of a work and its effect. Bion's O and K (1965, 1962a), for example, are clearly his distortions, which have their essence in his body of work; the correspondence of O and K to his essence follow ratios worked out laboriously to his specifications, not to anyone else's. The meaning of these terms *is in the correspondence*, not in the terms themselves; outside of this correspondence they are as meaningless as the letters "o" and "k" considered by themselves. They are not stencils; Bion's O is not a circle that can be traced anywhere.

Put another way: O and K, used outside of this original correspondence, are no longer O and K, for what is meant by O and K *is this correspondence*, and this correspondence is so unique as to be incapable of replication. O and K snatched from their home in Bion's oeuvre are merely distortions, which when transplanted into a foreign setting have no correspondence with the essence of their new environment. Displaced, they become either distortions disingenuously projected onto an unsuitable mirror or markers that palely and inadequately invoke the life that O and K had in their original setting. Of course, in taking an element out of the special conditions of its initial environment (where its relationship to some final corrected image had been honed with great labor) and setting it down anew in fresh surroundings, one will invariably find the ratio between distortions and mirror image to be different from that of the original environment. If the ratios are different, the distortion will not project a corrected image in its new setting.

Psychoanalytic criticism errs, then, if it thinks that its own distortions on the page can find a predictable, corrected image in a literary mirror. A psychoanalytic critic who coarsely applies the elements of psychoanalysis is merely using literature as a curved mirror on which to project psychoanalytic distortions, in the hope that the mirror of literature will reflect back an image that will appear to be a corrected image of the psychoanalytic essence. For example, to say that a novel has a "melancholic structure" is to project the psychoanalytic element "melancholia" onto a novel that has a curvature such that it will return, in a particularly clear form, the essence of the element. The novel serves as a device for turning what may feel like a vague distortion (the concept of melancholia) into a specific, recognizable instance (a corrected image, found in the text). Literature is reduced to a mirror with a desired, and entirely predictable, curvature onto which psychoanalysis can project a distortion in the hopes of getting a corrected essence. Such a reading is a projection of psychoanalysis, not a reading of literature. It presumes, against everything just said, that a corrected image can be reliably projected from a distortion, in this case a distortion that has the added disadvantage of having its natural essence in the setting of another work.

Criticism must have its own mirror, must understand that its initial distortions (its words, its interpretations) have a coherent essence in a mirror all its own. Each distortion must be adapted to its own curved mirror, which is the same as saying that when we write, if we wish to write in a way that retains our own critical essence, we must make our own distorted marks on the page, and figure out for ourselves what image we think we are casting in a mirror curved to our own requirements (as Jarrell remade tone in relation to his own cylindrical mirror). This, in most instances, will demand that we forego the distortions of others and make some of our own; in such a way, the unique event of literature is counterbalanced by a critical event. If in some cases elements are used, the critic must understand that they are not stencils that can be used to rapidly recreate an idea or concept.

Ultimately, criticism does not elevate itself into an art form unless it finds a way to be unpredictable, which is to be art itself. It cannot become art if it merely applies the distortions of others, or uses literature as a mirror in which to gaze at itself. Criticism, whether it be psychoanalytic criticism or some other form, can only become art if it works toward an unpredictable essence all its own.

Stereoscopic thinking: seeing in parallel

Criticism and art, understood as I have just described them, do not have a parasitic or symbiotic relationship; criticism is not leant against literature like a ladder against a house, needing it in order to get atop it. Criticism and art lead parallel lives. It is parallelism, not convergence, which imbues their co-existence with intellectual and artistic value. Criticism and art should be understood as having a relationship very much like that between the two, forward-facing eyes that we, as humans, posses. Consider the process by which we see the world: a distance of approximately three inches separates our eyes horizontally. As a result, each eye receives a slightly different two-dimensional picture of the world. If, for instance, you stare at the edge of a pyramid, your left eye will see more of the left side of the pyramid, the right eye see more of the right side of the pyramid. The images in the two eyes are different, creating what is called retinal disparity. It was for a long time a mystery how this retinal disparity was overcome to create a coherent binocularity in human vision. How can we see a single, solid world if all we perceive is two different, two-dimensional images?

In 1838, the British physicist Charles Wheatstone published a series of studies on binocularity, which for the first time grasped the critical point that retinal disparity is not an impediment to stereopsis, but is in fact necessary to it. Wheatstone began by making line drawings of the images of simple objects, as they were perceived by the left eye alone, and by the right eye alone. He then invented a device, called a stereo-scope, that could present these images together to the viewer; the left eye viewing only the left eye's image, the right eye viewing only the right eye's image. Viewed this way through the stereoscope, the objects would miraculously spring into three-dimensional relief (just as they do when looking through a child's View-Master), demonstrating that our sense of the solidity of objects comes from retinal disparity. The brain relies upon measuring the differences in the images taken in by each eye to create three-dimensional depth perception. A stereoscope is, really, an instrument that allows us to witness the coming together of parallel images into three-dimensionality, something that is happening for each of us effortlessly at every moment.

To look at criticism and art side by side should give one the experience of looking into the most marvelous of stereoscopes. The autonomy of each image— their respective essences—can still be studied independently or checked against one another, just as we always have the option of viewing criticism and art separately or applying one to the other. But our real pleasure is in watching the parallel images merge into a special relationship that grants them a depth, a vividness, a life-like-ness that they do not have when viewed singly, and could not have absent a mind capable of handling both their similarities and their disparities. When, in his memoirs, Henry James describes the lower Manhattan of his youth, his evocations of the most familiar places—Washington Square Park, Fourteenth Street—thrill the reader because of how the image of today's New York and the image of nineteenth-century New York are experienced by the reader stereoscopically; as the reviewer Adam Gopnik (2016) put it, the familiar landmarks of New York:

> all register as the places they are now and were then, and are dazzlingly unlike. We are both in a city we know and in another city entirely, bearing the same street names, and this double vision delights us on each page.

As with James' rendering of New York, the coming together of the critical and creative projects is to look through a stereoscope; in looking through it, one is afforded a position from which one can examine a process—the merging of irreducible reality with critical consideration—that is central to everyday human life, though rarely observed, for just as with vision, it is a process that is for the most part involuntary and invisible to us. Stereoscopic thinking, then, can come about not only through the appropriate pairing of a reader and a critic but also from the reader alone, if he can think in such a way that the critical aspect of mind is brought into a stereoscopic relationship with the part of mind that experiences the art in a less critical, more immediate fashion.

But art and criticism brought together in parallel—perhaps like patient and analyst working in parallel—allow us to study and take pleasure in the experience of what they together create without ever being allowed for a moment to believe that one image is an explanation for, or a reflection of, the other. One eye does not explain the other. They are closer to being what Carson McCullers describes to begin her novel: two mutes, always together. If we are aware that our relationship to art and criticism is stereoscopic, we also know that the appearance of solidity created by keeping art and criticism parallel to one another is simply appearance, a wonderful and enormously useful trick the mind does to recreate reality in an advantageous way. The three-dimensionality is a construction, one that we can only study and understand if we can also separate, at times, the combined images into separate images. Which is what we do much of the time: we leave art to one side, criticism to another, and on occasion we take up our stereoscope. This is as it should be; for only in granting art and criticism their independence—their retinal disparity—can we ever get the stereoscopic perspective from them that we desire. It is stereoscopic thinking that should determine how we conceive of the relationship of criticism and art to one another.

Psychoanalytic literary criticism, then, should not busy itself applying or attaching one field to the other, just as we would not want one eye to observe the other, causing us to become cross-eyed and blind. Instead, the critic must see psychoanalysis and literature as through a stereoscope: psychoanalysis in one eye, literature in the other. The role of the analytic critic is, in that case, two-fold. First, to think stereoscopically, which means thinking about the two fields not as explanations for the other but as unique images, which when viewed from a certain perspective turn out to offer up another dimension. And, second, to be the builder of wonderful stereoscopes. A work of criticism ought to hold a stereoscope up to the reader's eyes, granting the reader access to the stereopsis in which the critic sees. Criticism is a technology for seeing, one that illuminates the advantages and pleasures of the critic's unique stereoscope, and allows the reader to momentarily feel that the essence of art and the essence of criticism—the three-dimensional images on their curved mirrors—have come into view.

Consider, finally, a short fictional story, in which a man spends the whole of his life—day in, day out—writing fiction. Beginning at the age of twenty, he goes about his craft with steady, tireless devotion, without break, until the age of eighty.

He is educated, independently wealthy, widely read: nothing constrains him; he is able to give his entire life to writing. And yet, we discover, the man never gets better at writing. This is the mystery of the story. A man writes all the time, his entire life, but never improves at it; not by his own estimation, not in the eyes of the many friends and acquaintances he conscripts throughout his life to read his work. He was not a particular great writer at twenty years of age, or at thirty years of age; or at forty, or at fifty, sixty, seventy, eighty years. At everything else at which he works the man shows improvement, but never at writing.

It is easy to believe that the story raises one, all too obvious question: why does the man not improve? But that is not the question that the story raises. The real question is: what has the man actually been working at all these years? Where is the mirror—his mirror—the mirror he had not known was there, and on which something has been projected? This is where the critic must begin, and so it is also where I must stop.

Notes

1 This chapter is an abridged version of a keynote address delivered at the congress, "The Logics of Pleasure, the Ambiguity of Pain," held by the Italian Psychoanalytic Society, May 26–29 2016. The address was subsequently published in *La Rivista di Psicoanalisi* (2016).
2 I recall here, as I did in the preface, Winnicott, in "The Place where we Live": "I am attempting to get in between these two extremes. If we look at our lives we shall probably find that we spend most of our time neither in behaviour nor in contemplation, but somewhere else. I ask: where? And I try to suggest an answer" (1971, p. 105).
3 Jarrell here is quoting Housman's "Stars, I have seen them fall": "The toil of all that be/ Helps not the primal fault; It rains into the sea,/ And still the sea is salt" (1965, p. 166).

REFERENCES

Aalen, M. (2017). Stray thoughts – seeking home: Henrik Ibsen's *Peer Gynt* read in light of Wilfred Bion's ideas. *International Journal of Psychoanalysis*, 98: 415–434.

Akhtar, S. (2013). *Psychoanalytic listening: Methods, limits and innovations*. London: Karnac.

Amis, M. (2001). *The war against cliché: Essays and reviews 1971–2000*. New York: Vintage.

Aridjis, H. (1971/2016). *The child poet*. Trans. Chloe Aridjis. New York: Archipelago Books.

Barnes, J. (2015). *Keeping an eye open: Essays on art*. New York: Knopf.

Bergman, M. (2013). *The unconscious in Shakespeare's plays*. London: Karnac.

Berlin, L. (2015). *A manual for cleaning women*. New York: Farrar, Straus & Giroux.

Berman, J. (1990). *Narcissism and the novel*. New York: New York University Press.

Bion, W. R. (1962a). *Learning from experience*. New York: Basic Books.

Bion, W.R. (1962b). A theory of thinking. *International Journal of Psycho-Analysis* 43: 306–310.

Bion, W.R. (1965). *Transformations*. London: Heinemann.

Bion, W.R. (1991). *A memoir of the future*. London: Karnac.

Bishop, E. (1983). *The complete poems 1927–1979*. New York: Farrar, Straus & Giroux.

Bloom, H. (1982). Freud and the sublime: A catastrophe theory of creativity. In *Agon: Toward a Theory of Revisionism*. Oxford: Oxford University Press.

Bonaparte, M. (1949). *Edgar Poe, etude psychanalytique* [The life and works of Edgar Allan Poe: A psychoanalytic interpretation]. London: Imago. (First published 1933).

Borges, J.L. (1998). *Collected fictions*. Trans. Andrew Hurley. New York: Penguin.

Borges, J.L. (1999). *Selected poems*. New York: Penguin.

Borges, J.L. (2009). A dream. *The New Yorker*, July 6.

Brooks, P. (1984). *Reading for the plot: Design and intention in narrative*. New York: Knopf.

Brooks, P. (1994). *Psychoanalysis and storytelling*. London: Wiley-Blackwell.

Carrol, L. (1893). *Sylvie and Bruno concluded*. New York: Macmillan.

Casey, E. (1981). Sartre on imagination. In Paul Arthur Schlipp (ed.), *The philosophy of Jean-Paul Sartre*. Illinois: Open Court.

Civitarese, G. (2013). *The violence of emotions: Bion and post-Bionian psychoanalysis*. New York: Routledge.

Coetzee, J.M. (1980). *Waiting for the barbarians*. New York: Viking.

Coetzee, J.M. (1984). Truth in autobiography. Commencement address. University of Cape Town, South Africa.

Coetzee, J.M. (1985). *Life and times of Michael K*. New York: Viking.

Coetzee, J.M. ([1985]1992). Confession and double thoughts: Tolstoy, Rousseau, Dostoevsky. First published in *Comparative Literature* 37. Reprinted in D. Atwell (ed.), *Doubling the point: Essays and interviews* (pp. 251–293). Cambridge: Harvard University Press.

Coetzee, J.M. (1994). *The master of Petersburg*. New York: Viking.

Coetzee, J.M. (1999). *Disgrace*. New York: Penguin.

Coetzee, J.M. (2004). *Elizabeth Costello*. New York: Penguin.

Coetzee, J.M. (2008). *Diary of a bad year*. New York: Penguin.

Coetzee, J.M. and Auster, P. (2013). *Here and now: Letters 2008–2011*. New York: Viking.

Coetzee, J.M. and Kurtz, A. (2015). *The good story: Exchanges on truth, fiction, and psychoanalytic psychotherapy*. London: Harvill Secker.

Crews, F. (1966). *The sins of the father: Hawthorne's literary themes*. New York: Oxford University Press.

DeLillo, D. (1985). *White noise*. New York: Viking.

Dickinson, E. (2007). A loss of something ever felt I — . In *The poems of Emily Dickinson*. North Carolina: Hayes Barton Press.

Dostoevsky, F. ([1868]2003). *The Idiot*. Trans. R. Pevear and L. Volokhonsky. New York: Vintage.

Dostoevsky, F. ([1872]1994). *Demons*. Trans. R. Pevear and L. Volokhonsky. New York: Vintage.

Dostoevsky, F. ([1877]1997). The dream of a ridiculous man. In *The Eternal husband and other stories*. Trans. R. Pevear and L. Volokhonsky. New York: Bantam.

Ehrenzweig, A. (1971). *The hidden order of art*. Berkeley, CA: California University Press.

Eliot, G. (1990). *Selected essays, poems, and other writings*. New York: Penguin.

Felman, S. (1982). Turning the screw of interpretation. In *Literature and psychoanalysis: The question of reading: Otherwise*. Baltimore: Johns Hopkins University Press.

Forster, E.M. (1921). *Howard's end*. New York: Knopf.

Freud, S. (1908). *Creative writers and day-dreaming*. Standard Edition IX. London: Hogarth Press.

Freud, S. (1917). *On the history of the psycho-analytic movement, papers on metapsychology and other works (1914–1916)*. Standard Edition XIV. London: Hogarth Press.

Freud, S. (1918). *From the history of an infantile neurosis*. Standard Edition XVII. London: Hogarth Press.

Freud, S. (1930). *Civilization and its discontents*. Standard Edition XXI. London: Hogarth Press.

Frost, R. (1942/1995). Never again would birds' song be the same. In *Robert Frost: Collected poems, prose, & plays*. New York: Library of America.

Frost, R. (1969). Neither our far nor in deep. In *The poetry of Robert Frost: The collected poems*. New York: Henry Holt.

Fuller, P. (1981). *Art and psychoanalysis*. London and New York: Writers and Readers.

García Márquez, G. (1972). *Leaf storms and other stories*. Trans. Gregory Rabassa. New York: Harper & Row.

Gass, W.H. (1979). *Fiction & the figures of life*. Boston: David R. Godine.

Gopnik, A. (2016). Little Henry, happy at last. *The New Yorker*, January 16.

Greenacre, P. (1955). *Swift and Carroll: A psychoanalytic study of two lives*. New York: International Universities Press.

Griffin, F. (2016). *Creative listening and the psychoanalytic process: Sensibility, engagement, and envisioning*. London: Routledge.

Hawthorne, N. (1932). *The American notebooks*. Ed. Randall Stewart. New Haven, CT: Yale University Press.

Holland, N. (1968). *The dynamics of literary response* (1st edition). New York: Oxford University Press.

Houlding, S. (2015). Mourning in the psychoanalytic situation and in Shakespeare's *The Tempest*. *Psychoanalytic Quarterly* 84.1: 1–20.

Housman, A.E. (1965). *The collected poems of A.E. Housman*. New York: Henry Holt.

Irwin, J. (1980). Figurations of the writer's death. In *The literary Freud: Mechanisms of defense and the poetic will*. New Haven, CT: Yale University Press.

Ishiguro, K. (1982). *A pale view of hills*. London: Faber & Faber.

Ishiguro, K. (1986). *An artist of the floating world*. London: Faber & Faber

Ishiguro, K. (2005). *Never let me go*. New York: Vintage.

Ishiguro, K. (2008). *Conversations with Kazuo Ishiguro*. Jackson: University of Mississippi Press.

Jacobus, M. (2005). *The poetics of psychoanalysis in the wake of Klein*. Oxford: Oxford University Press.

James, H. (1991). *The turn of the screw*. New York: Dover.

James, W. (1890). *The principles of psychology*, vol. 1. New York: H. Holt.

Jarrell, R. (1999). To the Laodiceans. In *No other book: Selected essays*. Ed. B. Leithauser. New York: Harper Collins.

Johnson, B. ([1977]1982). The frame of reference: Poe, Lacan, Derrida. In S. Felman (ed.), *Literature and psychoanalysis: The question of reading: Otherwise*. Prev. pub. in *Yale French Studies*, 55/56. Baltimore: Johns Hopkins University Press.

Jones, E. (1949). *Hamlet and Oedipus*. New York: Norton.

Joyce, J. (1922). *A portrait of the artist as a young man*. New York: B.W. Huebsh.

Kafka, F. (1990). *Letters to Milena*. Trans. Philip Boehm. New York: Schocken Books.

Kentridge, W. (2014). *Six drawing lessons*. Cambridge, MA: Harvard University Press.

Kermode, Frank (1985). Can we say absolutely anything we like? In *The art of telling: Essays on fiction*. Cambridge, MA: Harvard University Press.

Kogan, I. (2014). Some reflections on Ian McEwan's Atonement: Enactment, guilt, and reparation. *Psychoanalytic Quarterly* 83.1: 49–70.

Köhler, W. (1925). *The mentality of apes*. London: Routledge.

Koolhaas, R. (1977). Life in the metropolis' or 'the culture of congestion. *Architectural Design* 47. 5. Reprinted in K.M. Hays (ed.), *Architectural theory since 1968*. Cambridge, MA: MIT Press, 1998.

Kris, E. (1952). *Psychoanalytic explorations in art*. New York: International Universities Press.

Laplanche, J.Pontalis, J.B. (1973). *The language of psychoanalysis*. London: Hogarth Press.

Lear, J. (1999). *Open minded: Working out the logic of the soul*. Cambridge, MA: Harvard University Press.

Lear, J. (2017). *Wisdom won from illness: Essays in philosophy and psychoanalysis*. Cambridge, MA: Harvard University Press.

Mahon, E. (2013). Betrayal as the creative force behind Oscar Wilde's *The Ballad of Reading Gaol*. In *Betrayal: Developmental, literary and clinical realms*. London: Karnac.

Manolopoulos, S. (2015). *Medea* by Euripides: Psychic constructions for preverbal experiences and traumas. *Psychoanalytic Quarterly* 84. 2: 441–461.

McClatchy, J.D. (1989). *White paper: On contemporary American poetry*. New York: Columbia University Press.

McCullers, C. (1940). *The heart is a lonely hunter*. Boston: Houghton Mifflin.

Meltzer, D. and Harris-Williams, M. (1988). *The apprehension of beauty: The role of aesthetic conflict in development, art and violence*. Harris Meltzer Trust.

Milner, M. (1950). *On not being able to paint*. London: Routledge.

Moss, D. (2012). *Thirteen ways of looking at a man: Psychoanalysis and masculinity*. New York: Routledge.

Nabokov, V. (1955). *Lolita*. New York: Putnam.

Nabokov, V. (1981). *Lectures on Russian literature*. Ed. Fredson Bowers. New York: Houghton Mifflin.

Nabokov, V. (1999). Nabokov's dreams. *The New Yorker*. March 29.

O'Connor, F. (1952). *Wise blood*. New York: Harcourt, Brace.

O'Connor, F. (1969). *Mystery and manners*. New York: Farrar, Straus, & Giroux.

O'Connor, F. (1971). *The complete short stories of Flannery O'Connor*. New York: Farrar, Straus, & Giroux.

Ogden, B.H. (2009). What philosophy can't say about literature: Stanley Cavell and *Endgame*. *Philosophy and Literature* 33. 1: 126–138.

Ogden, B.H. (2010). The coming into being of literature: How J.M. Coetzee's *Diary of a Bad Year* thinks through the novel. *NOVEL: A Forum on Fiction* 43. 3: 466–482.

Ogden, B.H. (2012a). Reconcile, reconciled: A new reading of reconciliation in J.M. Coetzee's *Disgrace*. *Ariel: A Review of International English Literature* 41. 3/4: 301–314.

Ogden, B.H. (2012b). Formal antagonisms: How Philip Roth writes Nathan Zuckerman. *Studies in American Fiction* 39.1: 87–101.

Ogden, B.H. (2013). The palimpsest of process and the search for truth in South Africa: How Phaswane Mpe wrote *Welcome to Our Hillbrow*. *Safundi: The Journal of South African and American Studies* 14.2: 191–208.

Ogden, B.H. (2014). Quantum criticism: A poetics of simultaneity for global literature. *Alif: Journal of Comparative Poetics* 34: 74–99.

Ogden, B.H. (2016). Review of *The Good Story: Exchanges on truth, fiction and psycho-analytic psychotherapy*. *Rivista di Psicoanalisi* 62.1: 149–167.

Ogden, B.H. (2017a). Bion and the apes: The bridging problem of *A Memoir of the Future*. In *Bion in contemporary psychoanalysis: Reading A Memoir of the Future*. New York: Routledge. •

Ogden, B.H. (2017b). The risk of true confession: On literature and mystery. *Fort da: Journal of the Northern California Society for Psychoanalytic Psychology* 23.1: 40–67. Originally in Portuguese, in *The represented and the unrepresented in psychic life*. Sao Paulo: Escuta.

Ogden, B.H. and Ogden, T.H. (2013). *The analyst's ear and the critic's eye: Rethinking psychoanalysis and literature*. New York andLondon: Routledge.

Petterson, P. (2005). *Out stealing horses*. New York: Picador.

Priel, B. (2011). Transcending the caesura: The reading effects of Borges's fiction. *International Journal of Psychoanalysis* 92. 6: 1617–1629.

Prose, F. (2013). Chasing the white rabbit. *New York Review of Books*, online. March 8.

Quasha, G. (2015). *The daimon of the moment: Preverbs*. Massachusetts: Talisman House.

Raab, L. (2009). The poem that can't be written. *The New Yorker*. April 6.

Roethke, T. ([1948]1975). The lost son. In *The collected poems of Theodore Roethke*. New York: Anchor Books.

Rose, G. (1980). *The power of form: A psychoanalytic approach to aesthetic form*. New York: International Universities Press.

Rousseau, J.-J. ([1782]1996). *The confessions*. Ed. T. Griffith, intro. D. Matravers. Ware, UK: Wordsworth Classics.

Ruiz, G. and Sánchez, N. (2014). Wolfgang Köhler's *The Mentality of Apes* and the animal psychology of his time. *Spanish Journal of Psychology* 17, e69: 1–25.

Ryle, G. (1949). *The concept of mind*. New York: Barnes & Noble.

Sartre, J.-P. ([1936]1962). *Imagination*. Trans. Forrest Williams. Ann Arbor, MI: University of Michigan Press.

Sartre, J.-P. ([1940]1962). *Psychology of imagination*. Trans. Bernard Frechtman. New York: Washington Square Press.

Schafer, R. (1994). *Retelling a life: Narration and dialogue in psychoanalysis*. New York: Basic Books.

Schiff, S. (1999). *Vera (Mrs. Vladimir Nabokov)*. New York: Random House.

Segal, H. (1952). A psychoanalytic approach to aesthetics. *International Journal of Psychoanalysis* 33: 196–207.

Segal, H. (1991). *Dream, phantasy and art*. New York: Routledge.

Stokes, A. (1965). *The invitation in art*. London: Tavistock Publications.

Tennyson, A. (1899). The two voices. In *The works of Alfred Lord Tennyson*, vol. 1. London: Macmillan.

Vesaas, T. ([1957]2016). *The birds*. New York: Archipelago Books.

Wallace, D.F. (1999). The depressed person. In *Brief interviews with hideous men*. New York: Little, Brown.

Wilson, E. (1976). The ambiguity of Henry James. In *The triple thinkers: Twelve essays on literary subjects*. New York: Farrar, Straus, & Giroux.

Winnicott, D.W. (1971). *Playing and reality*. New York: Basic Books.

Winnicott, D.W. (1974). Fear of breakdown. *International Journal of Psychoanalysis* 1: 103–107.

Woolf, V. (1932). *The second common reader*. New York: Harcourt.

INDEX

Note: italic page numbers indicate figures; page numbers followed by *n* indicate chapter endnote numbers.

CPSIA information can be obtained
at www.ICGtesting.com
Printed in the USA
LVHW082121160119
604153LV00011B/196/P

9 780815 377283